omnipotent
omniscient
mutable - changeable

WHAT IS GOD?

WHAT IS GOD?

The Selected Essays of
Richard R. La Croix

Edited by Kenneth G. Lucey

**PROMETHEUS
BOOKS**
Buffalo, New York

Published 1993 by Prometheus Books

97 96 95 94 93   5 4 3 2 1

Library of Congress Cataloging-in Publication Data

La Croix, Richard R.
    What is God? : selected essays of Richard R. La Croix / edited by Kenneth G. Lucey.
        p.   cm.
    Includes bibliographical references.
    ISBN 0-87975-739-6 (alk. paper)
    1. God—Attributes. I. Lucey, Kenneth G., 1942–   II. Title.
BT130.L24   1993
212—dc20   93-20193
                                                                    CIP

Printed in the United States of America on acid-free paper.

Contents

5

6   Contents

Synoptic Introduction

by Kenneth G. Lucey

The young Augustine is famous for his prayer which paraphrases roughly as "Give me strength, oh Lord, to resist these temptations of the flesh—but not just yet." In a similar vein, one can well imagine the young La Croix—very much a theist early on—praying in some such fashion as: "Give me the intellectual strength, oh Lord, to simplify the complexities of our concept of You—but not just yet." It is certainly the case that Richard R. La Croix has made a brilliant and highly productive career of exploring the conceptual intricacies of the Judeo-Christian concept of God. This collection includes twenty-one essays (three previously unpublished) spanning the period of 1972 through 1990 in which La Croix plumbs previously unrecognized or insufficiently explored depths of the concept of God. The essays in this volume are presented chronologically in order to display for the reader the dialectic of Professor La Croix's exploration of these subtleties.

In the first essay in this collection, "Malcolm's *Proslogion* III Argument," La Croix is discussing Norman Malcolm's work titled "Anselm's Ontological Argument," one of the most influential articles in the philosophy of religion produced in the twentieth century. In 1960 Malcolm set off philosophical earthquakes with his defense of a version of the ontological argument. In his response, La Croix musters his own reasons for thinking that Malcolm was wrong, and for believing that *Proslogion*

7

III does not contain a logically complete and independent argument for the proposition that something-than-which-a-greater-cannot-be-thought cannot be thought not to exist. La Croix also deploys reasons for doubting that this argument can be attributed to Anselm or is one to which he is committed to accepting as his own.

Essay two, "The Incompatibility of Omnipotence and Omniscience," is La Croix's first published encounter with the divine property of omnipotence. In this one-page essay La Croix posits that "it would appear to follow that a being who is both omnipotent and omniscient is logically impossible." The crux of the argument for this conclusion turns on the notion that an omnipotent being can create a finite being who performs an act known only to herself and to no other being, whereas an omniscient being cannot engage in such an act of creation. Hence, La Croix there concluded, no being could be both omnipotent and omniscient.

Essay three, "Omnipotence, Omniscience, and Necessity," which follows the previous effort by eight months, explores two possible responses to his previous argument's assertion of a logical incompatibility between the properties of omnipotence and omniscience. In the first of these responses La Croix makes a distinction between the properties of mutable and immutable omniscience. He there argues that the theist can establish the compatibility of omnipotence and omniscience only by embracing the notion that God is at best "mutably-omniscient."

The second response that La Croix explores is a line of reasoning by which his original argument (for the incompatibility of omnipotence and omniscience) fails. It envisions a possible world containing one omnipotent being and another (possibly distinct) immutably omniscient being. The response is that in such a world the omnipotent being cannot without contradiction create b (the being who does an act known only to herself). The problem that La Croix finds with this second response is that it is unavailable to any theist who believes that God's existence is logically necessary.

In essay four, "Unjustified Evil and God's Choice," La Croix turns his attention to chapters 5 and 6 of Alvin Plantinga's well-known book *God and Other Minds*. Here he is dealing with the classical problem of evil and the equally traditional free-will defense thereto. Plantinga's claim is that for the atheologian to succeed it must be shown that there is a set of propositions about God's goodness and the evil in the world such that each proposition in the set is either logically true or essential to theism and such that the set entails a contradiction. Plantinga challenges the atheologian to produce such a set and believes that none such is forth-coming. La Croix accepts the challenge and believes that the crucial proposition in such a set is that *God had the choice of not creating at all.* Building upon this key proposition, La Croix shows that there *is* a set *S* of exactly the sort that Plantinga required, and in the end La Croix concludes: "So it would appear that theism is inconsistent and that the theist must give up one or more of his claims about God."

In essay five, "God Might Not Love Us," the issue in question is how we should understand the traditional doctrine of God's immutability. La Croix is here engaging in further debate with Alvin Plantinga, and with James Tomberlin over the appropriate account of the concept of nonrelational properties as it occurs in the doctrine that God has all of His nonrelational properties essentially. La Croix faults Tomberlin's for-mulation on the grounds that it has the unhappy consequence that the property of loving everyone might turn out to be a property that God lacks, which of course no traditional theist could accept.

The proper account of the property of omnipotence has long been one of the most perplexing puzzles in the philosophy of religion. It is thus understandable that this is a topic to which La Croix returns several times in these essays from a variety of different perspectives. Essay six, "Swinburne on Omnipotence," is another such occasion. La Croix's subject is a very sophisticated account of omnipotence that has been developed by Richard Swinburne. La Croix faults Swinburne on two grounds, name-ly, (1) it is not completely successful in answering Plantinga's objection, which implies an agent is omnipotent which is capable of only scratching her ear, and (2) the analysis entails that if God is omnipotent, then He is not omniscient.

In essay seven, "Aquinas on the Self-Evidence of God's Existence," La Croix is investigating a distinction that Aquinas has made between two ways in which a proposition can be self-evident. Aquinas' thesis is this: the proposition that God exists is self-evident in the first way but is not self-evident in the second way. Aquinas' task is to show that the proposition being self-evident in the first sense does not trivialize the pro-gram of rational theology found in his five proofs for the existence of God. Aquinas' notion is that a proposition can be self-evident in itself but not self-evident to us. La Croix argues that Aquinas fails in this en-deavor because, he argues, the second way of being self-evident entails a contradiction.

In "Omniprescience and Divine Determinism," the eighth essay of this volume, La Croix is at pains to argue that the traditional properties of God, namely, that God is omniscient, has foreknowledge, is eternal, and is immutable, have the regrettable implication that God is a completely determined being. La Croix further argues that when these first four properties are supplemented with the notion that God decides to perform the acts which He does perform, then this set of properties taken as a whole is seen to be inconsistent and entails a contradiction. The key idea pervading this discussion is that there is a tension between the notions of divine immutability and the doctrine of divine foreknowledge of *all* future events, which La Croix calls the doctrine that God is omniprescient.

Essay nine, "The Impossibility of Defining 'Omnipotence',", begins by delineating four apparently uncontroversial necessary conditions that are required by any adequate definition of the divine property of omnipotence. They are: (1) it should not require that an omnipotent being be able to bring about a state of affairs that is logically impossible to bring about; (2) it should not require that an omnipotent being be able to bring about a state of affairs that is impossible for an omnipotent being to be able to bring about; (3) it should not be inconsistent with the other traditional divine properties, such as being omniscient, omnipresent, all-loving, etc.; and (4) it should not be too broad, in the sense of judging beings to be omnipotent which clearly are not omnipotent. La Croix locates his primary difficulties in a tension between the third and fourth conditions. He argues that every definition of 'omnipotence' that satisfies condition (3) is too broad and thus fails to satisfy (4); and every definition that satisfies (4) and is thus not too broad, fails to satisfy (3). Hence, La Croix argues, the inability of any definition to simultaneously satisfy the third and fourth conditions establishes the impossibility of defining omnipotence.

In essay ten, "The Hidden Assumption in the Paradox of Omnipotence," La Croix is discussing the most famous contemporary puzzle concerning the property of omnipotence, namely, the dilemma posed by the paradox of the stone. La Croix argues that the hidden assumption underlying the paradox of the stone is the assumption (A), namely: 'x is omnipotent' entails 'x can lift anything and x can create anything.' La Croix shows how even true instances of the form 'God cannot create O' need not count against divine omnipotence. So, at least in the case of this famous dilemma, La Croix argues, the paradox of omnipotence is no problem for theologians.

Essay eleven, "Augustine on the Simplicity of God," has La Croix grappling with the traditional doctrine that God is different from everything else in the world in that He is simple. La Croix explores Augustine's different accounts of what this doctrine amounts to. In the *City of God* simplicity is identified as the inability to lose any of the properties an entity possesses. Elsewhere Augustine explicates simplicity in terms of a distinction between relative properties and nonrelative properties. La Croix subtly investigates this latter distinction and concludes that it fails to provide us with a coherent account of the concept of divine simplicity. Beyond the consideration of simplicity, this essay is important as an exploration of a fundamental metaphysical distinction among properties.

Essay twelve, "Failing to Define 'Omnipotence,' " returns to the topic of essay nine and defends the conclusion reached there against an attempted refutation by Professor George Mavrodes. Mavrodes has proposed a definition of 'omnipotent being' that was supposed to avoid the incompatibility of the third and fourth necessary conditions. In this self-contained response La Croix argues that Mavrodes's definition fails for very much the same reasons evinced in essay nine.

Essay thirteen is entitled "Is There a Paradox of Omniscience?" In this article La Croix again appears as champion and defender of a divine attribute. In this case he is arguing against J. L. Cowan's contention that there is a paradox of omniscience that parallels the paradox of omnipotence discussed in essay ten above, i.e., the paradox of the stone. J. L. Cowan had maintained that both the properties of omnipotence and of omniscience entail contradictions. La Croix demonstrates that Cowan's argument does not apply to the concept of omniscience, and exhibits formally why the purported parallelism is only apparent, but not real.

Essay fourteen, "Wainwright, Augustine, and God's Simplicity: A Final Word" returns to the topic of essay eleven. William J. Wainwright has raised three objections to La Croix's critique of Augustine's account of divine simplicity. La Croix accepts Wainwright's first objection, but then shows that it is not serious in that slightly different counter-examples establish the same point. The crucial issue here is the Augustinean distinction between relative and nonrelative properties. Wainwright's second objection proposes a reformulation of the distinction, but La Croix argues that the new examples defeat the reformulated distinction as well. Wainwright's third and last objection offers a new interpretation of Augustine's doctrine of divine simplicity, but after a discussion of the Augustinean texts, La Croix concludes that "there is no reason to think that Wainwright's interpretation is any different from mine let alone preferable."

In essay fifteen, "Divine Omniprescience: Are Literary Works Eternal

Entities?" La Croix returns to one of the themes of essay eight, namely, the notion that God is omniscient concerning all future events. This quality has been called omniprescience. In this essay La Croix argues that this divine property is incompatible with the commonly held view that literary authorship is creative and arises from a composing activity. La Croix's view is that one must either give up the doctrine of divine omniprescience or else reject the opinion that literary works do not exist prior to the creative acts of the agents who author them. La Croix contends that the theist has either the problem of defending the claim that the future is unknowable or the problem of rejecting the traditional belief that God is omniscient. Also, La Croix explores the logical consequences of rejecting the doctrine of literary creativity.

Essay sixteen is entitled "Aquinas on God's Omnipresence and Time-lessness." Two doctrines essential to the theology of St. Thomas Aquinas are (1) the doctrine that God is omnipresent, and (2) the doctrine that God is eternal. Of the various interpretations of the doctrine that God is eternal, Aquinas opts for the view that it is of the very essence of God that He is timeless in the sense of being neither in time nor subject to literal temporal predications. In this essay La Croix argues that the doctrine of divine omnipresence requires that temporal predications do actually apply to Him. La Croix raises doubts that Aquinas has succeeded in making a genuine distinction between the temporal and the timeless, and in the end concludes that two doctrines essential to Aquinas' rational theology are logically incompatible.

In essay seventeen, "Descartes on God's Ability to Do the Logically Impossible," La Croix is challenging the highly influential interpretation of Descartes that has been propounded by Harry Frankfurt. Philosophers have held as a standard that no account of divine omnipotence is adequate if it entails that God can do the logically impossible. Frankfurt credits Descartes with believing otherwise. In this important essay, La Croix offers a different interpretation of the passages cited by Frankfurt, and argues that these passages do not support the Frankfurt interpretation. The issue here centers upon Descartes' caution against thinking that "God's power is determined by something independent of Him rather than that His power is self-determined and absolute. . . ." La Croix concludes that if Descartes' account of divine omnipotence is incoherent, it is incoherent for reasons other than that it entails the possibility of doing what is logically impossible.

Essay eighteen, "The Paradox of Eden," is the last of the previously published essays in this volume. It is a small gem of less than four hundred words aimed directly at every fundamentalist who ever maintained that the Bible is a literally true recitation of divine dictation. More precisely, the target here is Genesis 3:16–19. La Croix is concerned to raise a difficulty with the story of Adam and Eve eating of the tree of the knowledge of good and evil. The essay has the overall logical form of a complex constructive dilemma, the general consequence of which is that "being just is *not* a necessary or essential property of God."

Essay nineteen is entitled "Divine Omniprescience: Can an Effect Precede Its Cause?" In this essay La Croix returns again to the doctrine that God is omniscient with regard to all future events, which doctrine La Croix calls divine omniprescience, and displays yet another untoward consequence thereof. Renewing a theme discussed in essay fifteen, La Croix discusses the ontology of a wide range of human compositions: literary, musical, dramatic, etc. His target here is the cause/effect relationship where the act of a human agent is the cause and the human composition is the effect. La Croix's conclusion is that given a set of traditional theological assumptions about God's omniscience, immutability, and temporality, it clearly follows that with regard to the whole set of human compositions, taken as effects, their existence necessarily precedes that of their cause. So, La Croix answers the question of his title in the affirmative—effects can precede their causes.

Essay twenty, "Metatheism," is the penultimate article in this volume and the only one with a purely methodological orientation. In this essay La Croix is meditating upon his previous two decades of thought and writing about the attributes of the Judeo-Christian deity and attempting to characterize his own unique position to stand alongside the traditional positions of the theist, the atheist, and the agnostic. This fourth stance La Croix calls "metatheism" and as a holder of that position he calls himself a "metatheist." La Croix views this stance as an outgrowth of logical positivism. The overriding concern of the metatheist is the philosophical investigation of the meaning of the sentence "God exists." Unlike the logical positivist, La Croix is not concerned with some *general* criterion for the meaningfulness of *all* sentences, but rather is concerned with the quite particular meanings associated with the specific sentence "God exists."

As La Croix views the matter, the theist, the atheist, and the agnostic all share the common assumption that the sentence "God exists" is meaningful, and given that assumption their common concern is with the truth-value of that sentence. The metatheist questions that common assumption and takes his primary task to be the investigation of what the meaning of the sentence "God exists" might be. The metatheist is unwilling to accept the assumption as legitimate without further justification. Rather, he requires that the meaning of the sentence "God exists" be stated and explicated. La Croix's explicit complaint is that theists, atheists, and agnostics never do in fact state explicitly and completely what the sentence "God exists" means and it is not at all clear that they all mean the same thing by the sentence.

In terms of the issue of the goodness of God La Croix goes on to make a case for the contention that the sentence "God exists" simply has no common meaning for all theists, let alone for all theists, atheists, and agnostics. By La Croix's lights the most important task for the metatheist is the attempt to *discover* or *uncover* the assumed meaning of the sentence "God exists" for the purpose of establishing some ground for making a judgment about the truth-value of that sentence. Unfortunately, La Croix asserts, the theist never provides an explicit understandable meaning for the sentence "God exists." So the metatheist turns instead to his next best question, namely: What is God? (hence the title of this collection). Thus, the metatheist makes his focus the theist's explicit claims about the nature and properties of God, such as omnibenevolence, omnipotence, omniscience, immutability, etc. These claims by the theist are taken as partial explications of the meaning of the sentence "God exists."

La Croix devotes the rest of this essay to showing that there are a number of complications besetting the metatheist's endeavor. In the process he calls upon a number of points made in the preceding essays of this volume, such as the issues raised by temporality and omnipresence in essay sixteen.

One of the major conclusions that La Croix arrives at in this essay is that in order for the metatheist to get to the stage of making an absolute judgment about the sentence "God exists" it is required that he identify a partial meaning of the sentence that is demonstrably necessary for *all* versions of theism. In that sense La Croix views essays ten and seventeen as metatheistic defenses of theism. In the same sense essay four is a metatheistic attack upon theism. But in each case this holds only to the extent to which it be granted that one or another property really is a necessary condition for all versions of theism.

Essay twenty-one, "The Problem of Evil and Augustine's Account of Human Free Will and Divine Grace," is the final essay of this volume and the most recent of La Croix's writings in the philosophy of religion. The problem of evil is the single most important of the nontheists' arguments for the nonexistence of God. In this essay La Croix brings a whole new perspective to this much discussed topic. La Croix shows that the problem of evil for Augustine is a very different matter. The contemporary problem of evil centers upon human suffering, whereas for Augustine human suffering is not even considered an evil. Instead, for Augustine, the problem of evil centers upon Adam's fall from grace. This leads La Croix into a discussion of Augustine's account of human free will and three central principles concerning it. Also into this discussion enters Augustine's distinction between two kinds of grace. La Croix extracts from this mix of principles and distinctions an astute critique of Augustine's own unique theodicy. La Croix argues that Augustine's theory falls prey to an infinite regress argument, which in the end leaves his view inconsistently entailing a contradiction, a situation that at bottom causes La Croix to judge Augustine's theodicy to be a failure.

1

Malcolm's *Proslogion* III Argument

Eleven years ago Norman Malcolm claimed that *Proslogion* III contains an argument for the existence of God which is distinguishable from the argument in *Proslogion* II.[1] According to Professor Malcolm, these two arguments are distinguishable by virtue of the fact that the argument in *Proslogion* III is both logically complete and independent of the argument in *Proslogion* II, and by virtue of the fact that the argument in *Proslogion* II has as its conclusion the claim

(G1) God exists

while the argument in *Proslogion* III has as its conclusion the stronger claim

(G2) God *necessarily* exists.

Malcolm admitted that there is no evidence that Anselm thought of himself as offering two different proofs.

If I understand Malcolm correctly, then what he is saying is that *Proslogion* III does in fact contain a logically complete and independent argument even though Anselm was unaware of the fact and that Anselm is committed to that argument despite the fact that he did not intend to provide it. I do not know if Malcolm still maintains these views, but

I thank E. J. Brill, Leiden, Netherlands, for allowing me to publish this paper which is part of an argument that appears in my book, *Proslogion II and III: A Third Interpretation of Anselm's Argument* (1972).

I think that they are mistaken. I think that neither *Proslogion* II nor *Proslogion* III contains a logically complete and independent argument, but that these two chapters have to be taken together in Anselm's programme in the *Proslogion;* but I will not attempt to argue those points here. Instead, I will argue a much narrower point. I will try to show that the argument which Malcolm identifies in *Proslogion* III cannot be attributed to Anselm.

If Malcolm is correct in his views, then we would expect to find in *Proslogion* III both the conclusion (G2) and a set of premises in support of (G2). But, as a matter of fact, we do not find (G2) as the conclusion of the reasoning in *Proslogion* III. What Anselm says is:

> And certainly this being so truly exists that it cannot be even thought not to exist. For something can be thought to exist that cannot be thought not to exist, and this is greater than that which can be thought not to exist. Hence, if that-than-which-a-greater-cannot-be-thought can be thought not to exist, then that-than-which-a-greater-cannot-be-thought is not the same as that-than-which-a-greater-cannot-be-thought, which is absurd. *Something-than-which-a-greater-cannot-be-thought exists so truly, then, that it cannot be even thought not to exist.*[2] (Italics mine.)

Now, if there is an argument going on here at all, whether logically complete or not, then the conclusion of this argument is stated in the first sentence and is repeated again in the final sentence, but the conclusion is not (G2). Instead Anselm concludes the reasoning in *Proslogion* III with the far more complex statement that something-than-which-a-greater-cannot-be-thought exists so truly that it cannot be even thought not to exist. This statement clearly makes at least two claims about Anselm's being, for it asserts *both* that

(a) Something-than-which-a-greater-cannot-be-thought exists

and that

(b) Something-than-which-a-greater-cannot-be-thought cannot be thought not to exist.

But Anselm's concluding statement also makes a third claim. It asserts that the being exists *so truly* that it cannot be thought not to exist. The force of the phrase "so truly" in this statement is that not only is it a fact that some being exists, and not only is it a fact that this being cannot be thought not to exist, but also the being's existence corresponds to the fact that it cannot be thought not to exist, that is, that

(c) Something-than-which-a-greater-cannot-be-thought cannot not exist.

If there is any doubt that this is Anselm's meaning, we have only to consult the *Reply* where Anselm explicitly distinguishes these three claims from one another and indicates that each one is deducible in his proof. In chapter V of the *Reply* Anselm says:

> Thus, if anyone should say that 'that-than-which-a-greater-cannot-be-thought' is not something that actually exists, or that it can possibly not exist, or even can be thought of as not existing, he can easily be refuted. . . . It is evident, then, that it neither does not exist nor can not exist or be thought of as not existing.[3]

In short, we do not find (G2) in *Proslogion* III, as we would expect to from what Malcolm tells us about *Proslogion* III. Rather, Anselm concludes the reasoning of *Proslogion* III with the far more complex claim that something-than-which-a-greater-cannot-be-thought exists, cannot be thought not to exist, and cannot not exist, that is, the complex claim (a)-(b)-(c). Furthermore, even a cursory reading of the reasoning of *Proslogion* III should make it plain that the two sentences that would have to be the premises of this alleged argument are not strong enough to support the conclusion (a)-(b)-(c).

But if in (b) of (a)-(b)-(c) we substitute the term 'God' for the term 'something-than-which-a-greater-cannot-be-thought' and if, as Malcolm does, we transform Anselm's phrase "cannot be thought not to exist" into either the phrase "logically impossible not to exist" or the phrase "necessarily exists," then Anselm's conclusion (a)-(b)-(c) becomes (a)-(G2)-(c). Perhaps, after all, it can be maintained that *Proslogion* III does contain (G2), and that even though the premises are not sufficient to support Anselm's actual conclusion (a)-(b)-(c), they are sufficient to support the conclusion (G2). Even though Malcolm does not identify (a) and (c) of Anselm's conclusion and even though *Proslogion* III does not contain a logically complete and independent argument whereby the conclusion (a)-(b)-(c) is deducible, perhaps Malcolm is, after all, by virtue of his transformations, correct in claiming that *Proslogion* III contains a logically complete and independent argument whereby the conclusion (G2) is deducible.

However, Malcolm's view that (G2) is deducible from *Proslogion* III alone rests on two assumptions. First, it rests on the assumption that (b) is deducible from *Proslogion* III alone. Second, it rests on the assumption that Anselm's phrase "cannot be thought not to exist" is legitimately transformable into "logically impossible not to exist" or "necessarily exists" so that (b) is transformable into (G2), and any propositions implying (b) are transformable into propositions implying (G2). Consequently, the claim that *Proslogion* III contains a logically complete and independent argument whose conclusion is (G2)—an argument to which Anselm is committed despite the fact that he did not intend to provide such an argument—reduces to the claim that Anselm is committed to the indicated transformations and that (b) is deducible from *Proslogion* III alone. But even if it is true that (b) is deducible from *Proslogion* III alone, (G2) is not deducible in any way that would preserve an accurate representation of Anselm's intentions because there are crucial objections to transforming Anselm's phrase "cannot be thought not to exist" in the indicated way required to deduce (G2). When these objections are taken together they render highly unconvincing the view that (b) is legitimately transformable into (G2).

The first objection to this transformation of Anselm's phrase is that while it may be true that "x is logically impossible" entails "x cannot be thought" and, hence, that Malcolm's (G2) entails Anselm's (b), it is not at all obvious that "x cannot be thought" entails "x is logically impossible" and, hence, that Anselm's (b) entails Malcolm's (G2). If the first entailment holds it is because being logically possible is a condition of thought. But perhaps being logically possible is not the only condition of thought. Perhaps there are causal and psychological conditions of thought such that "x cannot be thought" might be true while "x is logically impossible" might be false. In order to maintain the view that Anselm is *logically* committed to this transformation, one would have to show that this second entailment holds.

The second objection to this transformation of Anselm's phrase was raised by Professor Gareth Matthews in an article responding to Malcolm's interpretation of Anselm.[4] In his article Matthews points out that Malcolm does not make a general practice of interpreting Anselm's phrase *"posse cogitari"* in terms of logical possibility and that there is a good reason not to do so. In chapter XV of the *Proslogion* Anselm says that God is "something greater than can be thought" and Matthews argues:

> Presumably Anselm means that God exceeds our powers of comprehension, not that God is greater than is logically possible (and therefore, presumably, logically impossible).[5]

The point, of course, is that chapter XV of the *Proslogion* provides evidence to suggest that this transformation of Anselm's phrases does not represent the meaning which Anselm intended to express in the original phrase. Now, if there is any doubt that "x is greater than is logically possible" ought to be rendered as "x is logically impossible" that doubt could only be raised on the ground that it is not at all clear that "x is greater than is logically possible" has any meaning at all. In either case, in order to maintain the view that Anselm is committed to Malcolm's transformation, one would have to be willing to allow that in chapter XV Anselm intended either to assert that God is logically impossible or to put forward a meaningless statement.

It would not do to suggest that *Proslogion* III is a special case where such a transformation ought to be performed because there is still one final objection which precludes even this possibility. We have already seen that Anselm clearly distinguishes claims (a), (b), and (c) from one another as separate and distinct claims about something-than-which-a-greater-can-not-be-thought. For Anselm (b) and (c) are clearly not alternative ways of asserting the same thing. Now, if the transformation of Anselm's ter-minology in terms of necessity and logical possibility is legitimate and appropriate at all, it is surely Anselm's term "cannot not exist" (*non potest non esse*) and not his term "cannot be thought not to exist" (*non possit cogitari non esse*) that should be so transformed.

But even in the case of claim (c) the legitimacy of such a transformation is highly dubious because Malcolm's transformation involves the notion of *logical* necessity and *logical* impossibility and it is not at all clear that Anselm means "logically impossible" by his term "*non posse non.*" Rather, in *Reply* VIII, *Proslogion* XIII, and *Proslogion* XIX Anselm indicates that to say that the being cannot not exist is to say that it has neither beginning nor end, that it is timeless and eternal, and that it is not in place or time. Consequently, even in Anselm's claim (c) there is no reason to suppose that he is asserting logically necessary existence of something-than-which-a-greater-cannot-be-thought, and it is a fiction to maintain the view that the transformation of Anselm's term "cannot be thought not to exist" into either the term "nonexistence is logically impossible" or the term "necessarily exists" represents the meaning of what Anselm intended to express in *Proslogion* III. Even if *Proslogion* III contains an uninten-tional but logically complete and independent argument which has as its conclusion (b), it does not contain a logically complete and independent argument which has as its conclusion (G2) because (b) cannot be legitimately transformed into (G2).

But now is there a logically complete and independent argument at all in *Proslogion* III? Is even claim (b) deducible from what would have to be the premises of *Proslogion* III if it contains a logically complete and independent argument? Malcolm represents the alleged *Proslogion* III argument in the following way:

> Anselm is saying . . . *that a being whose nonexistence is logically impossible is "greater" than a being whose nonexistence is logically possible* (and therefore that a being a greater than which cannot be conceived must be one whose nonexistence is logically impossible) . . . (Italics mine.)[6]

Presumably Malcolm reads the second sentence of *Proslogion* III as

(1) a being that cannot be thought not to exist is greater than a being that can be thought not to exist,

and by transforming Anselm's phrase "cannot be thought not to exist" into the phrase "nonexistence is logically impossible" and Anselm's phrase "can be thought not to exist" into the phrase "nonexistence is logically possible" he transforms what he takes to be Anselm's second sentence into "a being whose nonexistence is logically impossible is greater than a being whose nonexistence is logically possible." But not only does Malcolm's transformation misrepresent Anselm's reasoning, it is not at all clear that his reading of Anselm's second sentence in *Proslogion* III accurately represents Anselm's reasoning. If Malcolm would have us understand (1) to mean

(1a) for any x, if x cannot be thought not to exist then x is greater than what can be thought not to exist

then even if (b) is deducible from Malcolm's premise (1a) that deduction could not be represented as Anselm's argument because Anselm does not assert (1a) in *Proslogion* III. What Anselm says is:

> For something can be thought to exist that cannot be thought not to exist, and this is greater than that which can be thought not to exist.[7]

Now Anselm certainly says that something is greater than what can be thought not to exist, but he does not say that *if* something cannot be thought not to exist then it is greater than what can be thought not to exist. Rather, what Anselm says is that something can be thought to exist that cannot be thought not to exist, and it is this which is greater than what can be thought not to exist. Consequently, if Malcolm would have us understand (1) to mean (1a) then the argument which Malcolm identifies in *Proslogion* III cannot be attributed to Anselm.

If *Proslogion* III is to be interpreted as containing an unintentional but logically complete and independent argument whose conclusion is (b), then the premises of that argument must be

(2) Something, x, can be thought to exist and cannot be thought not to exist,

and

(3) x is greater than what can be thought not to exist.

But perhaps Malcolm would have us understand his premise (1) to mean

(1b) something, x, cannot be thought not to exist and x is greater than what can be thought not to exist.

Now it would appear that (1b) is substantially the same as the conjunction of Anselm's (2) and (3) except that (1b) does not contain the further claim that x can be thought to exist. This difference could be easily remedied. But if Malcolm would have us understand (1) to mean (1b), and if (1b) is substantially the same as the conjunction of Anselm's (2) and (3), then while it is possible to deduce (b) from (1b) because it is possible to deduce (b) from Anselm's (2) alone, that deduction is so trivial that there is no apparent reason to treat it as an argument.

This becomes apparent if we keep in mind that the primary assumption upon which all of Anselm's reasoning rests is the assumption that something-than-which-a-greater-cannot-be-thought can be thought to exist. This assumption is asserted in *Proslogion* II and in almost every chapter of the *Reply*. In fact in some chapters of the *Reply* it is asserted repeatedly. It is an assumption which is absolutely necessary to the entire structure of Anselm's reasoning, and if we do not at least provisionally accept that assumption, then Anselm's reasoning does not even get under way. In addition, it must be realized that Anselm explicitly states in *Reply* IV that something-than-which-a-greater-cannot-be-thought is unique as that which cannot be thought not to exist. Because of these facts it should be apparent that for Anselm the term "something-than-which-a-greater-cannot-be-thought" is the only term which can be substituted for x in (2) and (3) which yields true statements. So, for Anselm (2) is equivalent to

(2′) Something-than-which-a-greater-cannot-be-thought can be thought to exist, and cannot be thought not to exist,

and (3) is equivalent to

(3′) Something-than-which-a-greater-cannot-be-thought is greater than what can be thought not to exist.

Now if (1b) is substantially the same as the conjunction of Anselm's (2) and (3) then (1b) is equivalent to

(1b′) Something-than-which-a-greater-cannot-be-thought cannot be thought not to exist and is greater than what can be thought not to exist.

So, if (1b) is substantially the same as the conjunction of Anselm's (2) and (3), then while it is possible to deduce (b) from (1b′) and (2′) and, hence, from (1) and (2), that deduction is so trivial that there is no reason to treat it as an argument to which Anselm is committed. Since there is no evidence that Anselm thought of himself as offering two different proofs, there would seem to be no reason to treat the *possible* deduction of (b) from (2) as an argument presented by Anselm in *Proslogion* III, and since the deduction of (b) from (2) is so trivial there would seem to be no reason to treat the *possible* deduction of (b) from (2) as an argument unnoticed by Anselm, but nevertheless, present in *Proslogion* III. On the other hand, if (1b) is *not* substantially the same as the conjunction of Anselm's (2) and (3) then even if (b) is deducible from (1b) in a way that is not trivial that deduction does not represent an argument to which Anselm is committed since Anselm would not then be committed to (1b). In either case, then, it appears that *Proslogion* III does not contain a logically complete and independent argument for even assertion (b), at least not any argument that can be attributed to Anselm or one to which he is committed to accepting as his own.

NOTES

1. Norman Malcolm, "Anselm's Ontological Arguments," *Philosophical Review* 69 (January 1960): 41–62.
2. *St. Anselm's Proslogion with a Reply on Behalf of the Fool by Gaunilo and the Author's Reply to Gaunilo,* trans. with an introduction and philosophical commentary by M. J. Charlesworth (Oxford: Clarendon Press, 1965), p. 119.

3. Ibid., pp. 179–81.
4. Gareth B. Matthews, "On Conceivability in Anselm and Malcolm," *Philosophical Review* 70 (January 1961): 110–11.
5. Ibid., p. 110.
6. Malcolm, p. 45.
7. Anselm, p. 119.

2

The Incompatibility of
Omnipotence and Omniscience

Consider a finite (not omnipotent and not omniscient) being b and an act a such that b has as some of its self-consistent properties the properties ascribed in the statements:

(1) b does a

(2) b is the *only* being who knows that (1) is true.

Now, if 'x is omnipotent' entails

(3) x can create any finite being y, provided (i) y has properties such that the statement that y has those properties neither is self-contradictory nor entails a contradiction and (ii) there is no being z such that the statement that z and y exist either is self-contradictory or entails a contradiction,

then an omnipotent being can create b because the statement that b has the properties described in (1) and (2) does not appear to be self-contradictory or to entail a contradiction, and a can be an act and b a being such that the existence of b is consistent with the existence of all other existing beings. An omnipotent being *can* create a being who performs an act known only to himself and to no other being.

From *Analysis* 33, no. 5 (April 1973): 176. Copyright © 1973 by Richard R. La Croix. Reprinted by permission of the author and publisher.

But, if 'x is omniscient' entails

(4) For any finite being B and for any act A, if B does A then x knows that B does A,

then an omniscient being cannot create b. If an omniscient being created b then by (1) b does a and by (2) the omniscient being does *not* know that b does a and is, hence, not omniscient. An omniscient being *cannot* create a being who performs an act known only to himself and to no other being.

Since an omnipotent being *can* create b and an omniscient being *cannot* create b then 'x is omnipotent and omniscient' entails

(5) x can create b and x cannot create b.

But, since (5) is self-contradictory it would appear to follow that a being who is both omnipotent and omniscient is logically impossible.

3

Omnipotence, Omniscience, and Necessity

In "The Incompatibility of Omnipotence and Omniscience" (*Analysis* vol. 33, no. 5 [1973]) I argued that an omniscient being cannot create a finite being, *b,* who performs an act known only to himself and to no other being because an omniscient being must know about every act performed by every finite being. I also argued that an omnipotent being could create *b* and that, hence, no being can be both omnipotent and omniscient. I am no longer convinced that the argument can be sustained, because I have found two ways of escaping that argument. Professor Godbey, also, has noticed the second of them (see the preceding article in this journal[1]), but he does not draw what seems to me to be a consequence of this way of escaping the argument. For both of these possible escapes expose a fundamental difficulty in the view ascribable to some, though perhaps only a minority, of the exponents of traditional theism, that God is both a *logically* necessary being and immutable with respect to being omniscient. Further, this latter problem can be stated without considering the rather difficult question of whether or not *logical* necessity is a property *only* of propositions.

Let us say that a being is *mutably-omniscient* if and only if at some time or other he knows everything there is to be known at that time *and* it is possible that there be some other time either prior to or posterior to the time in question at which there is something he does not know.

From *Analysis* 34, no. 2 (December 1973): 63–64. Copyright © 1973 by Richard R. La Croix. Reprinted by permission of the author and publisher.

We will say that a being is *immutably-omniscient* if and only if he knows everything at every moment in time *and* it is impossible for him to ever fail to know anything. Now a mutably-omniscient being could create, say at T_1, a being, b, who performs an act known only to himself and to no other being, because b must obviously perform the act at some time, T_2, posterior to the time, T_1, of his creation. Of course, once b has performed the act in question our mutably-omniscient being is no longer omniscient. The point, though, is that the mutably-omniscient being could create b *while* possessing the property of being omniscient. So, a being can be both omnipotent and omniscient and my argument fails on the ground that an omniscient being can create b.

But on this ground my argument fails only if the being is omnipotent and *mutably*-omniscient. Clearly an *immutably*-omniscient being could not create b, and traditional theism, it would appear, requires the notion of immutable omniscience. As I understand traditional theism, God is omniscient, and omniscience is not a property He can possess at one time and not at another time. So the traditional theist cannot escape my argument by claiming that an omniscient being can create b even though the claim is true. However, the traditional theist can escape my argument by a different route.

I characterized an omnipotent being, *in part,* as one who can create any finite being y provided there is no being z such that the statement that z and y exist either is self-contradictory or entails a contradiction. But consider a universe in which there exists an omnipotent being and a being who is immutably-omniscient (perhaps the beings are identical, perhaps not). In such a universe an omnipotent being could *not* create b because the statement that an immutably-omniscient being and b exist entails a contradiction. So, in such a universe a being could be both omnipotent *and* immutably-omniscient and my argument fails on the ground that an omnipotent being *cannot* create b, if there is an immutably-omniscient being. Of course, the traditional theist could identify the universe in question with our own.

However, it would also appear to be the case that in our universe the existence of a finite being, b, who performs an act known only to himself and to no other being is a logically possible state of affairs. So, if there is an immutably-omniscient being, then the non-existence of that being must be a logically possible state of affairs. The existence of an immutably-omniscient being cannot be logically necessary or else the existence of a being b, who performs an act known only to himself and to no other being, is logically impossible, and I can see no reason to think that the existence of *b* is logically impossible.

So it would appear to follow that if my original argument is rejected on the first ground, then traditional theism must admit to a God who is mutably-omniscient; and if it is rejected on the second ground, then traditional theism cannot accept the claim that God's existence is logically necessary. My original argument cannot be rejected for either of these reasons without also rejecting the claim that God is both a being whose existence is logically necessary and immutable with respect to being omniscient.

NOTE

1. *Analysis* 34, no. 2 (December 1973): 62.

4

Unjustified Evil and God's Choice

In chapter 5 of *God and Other Minds* Alvin Plantinga has critically examined some recent attempts to show that the fact of evil renders traditional theistic belief self-contradictory.[1] He argues that these attempts are unsuccessful and claims that success is more difficult than most atheologians seem to suppose. I want to discuss Plantinga's examination in an attempt to show that the atheologian has not exhausted his arsenal and that the theist needs further defensive weapons in order to sustain his position that theistic belief is not irrational.

Plantinga maintains, and I believe correctly, that in order for the atheologian to show that theistic belief is self-contradictory it would be necessary to identify a set of propositions which both entails a contradiction and is such that each proposition in the set is either necessarily true, or essential to theism, or a logical consequence of such propositions. Clearly no set of propositions would present a problem for the theist if he were not committed, on some grounds or other, to each proposition in the set or if the set did not entail a contradiction. Furthermore, Plantinga maintains that the atheologians he is criticizing identify the set of propositions, (a) that God exists, (b) that God is omnipotent, (c) that God is omniscient, (d) that God is wholly good, and (e) that evil exists, as the set of propositions which is essential to orthodox theism and which is self-contradictory. But, Plantinga argues, while (a)–(e) is a set of propositions essential to theism, that set does not alone *formally* entail a contradiction.

From *Sophia* 13, no. 1 (April 1974): 20–28. Reprinted by permission.

Plantinga argues that in order to show that theism is self-contradic-tory the atheologian must add some further proposition to (a)–(e) and that the additional proposition must also be either necessarily true, or essential to theism, or a logical consequence of such propositions. Now it is quite plain that the additional proposition needed by the atheologian must satisfy a further condition: it must be a proposition which specifies the conditions under which a person can permit evil without forfeiting his claim to moral goodness. After examining several formulations of such a proposition and rejecting them either because they were not adequate for the atheologian's need, or because they failed to satisfy the condition of being necessarily true, or essential to theism, or a logical consequence of such propositions, Plantinga claims that at least part of the proposition the atheologian needs is the proposition that

(f$_4$) An omnipotent, omniscient person is wholly good only if he eliminates every evil which is such that for every good that entails it, there is a greater good that does not entail it.[2]

But Plantinga finds difficulties with this proposition as well. He points out that the conjunction of (a)–(e) and (f$_4$) is not a formally contradictory set either, because it does not entail the denial of (e), that is, it does not entail that there is no evil at all. Rather, that set of propositions entails

(g) Every evil E is entailed by some good G such that every good greater than G also entails E.

So, since the conjunction of (a)–(e) and (f$_4$) does not entail a contradiction, the addition of (f$_4$) to (a)–(e) is not by itself sufficient to show that theism is self-contradictory. The atheologian must add still another proposition to this set and this new proposition must be either necessarily true, or essential to theism, or a logical consequence of such propositions such that when it is added to the set the entire set entails the denial of (g):

There is at least one evil state of affairs such that for every good that entails it, there is a greater good that does not.

According to Plantinga, then, the atheologian can convict the theist of inconsistency only if he can deduce the denial of (g) from (a)–(e) and (f$_4$) together with propositions which are either necessarily true, or essential to theism, or logical consequences of such propositions because since it is (g) and not the denial of (e) which is entailed by (a)–(e) and (f₄), theism can be shown to be self-contradictory only if it is possible to deduce the contradictory conjunction of (g) and the denial of (g) by deducing the denial of (g) in the specified way. Furthermore, Plantinga indicates that if the atheologian can deduce the denial of (g) and we can say that an evil state of affairs is *justified* just in case it is false that for every good that entails it there is a greater good that does not, then the atheologian will have succeeded in showing that there is unjustified evil because the denial of (g) says that there is at least one evil state of affairs such that for every good that entails it there is a greater good that does not.[3]

Plantinga continues this phase of his examination with an honest but unsuccessful attempt to find a proposition which satisfies the necessary conditions for the deduction of the denial of (g) and concludes by saying, "If this does not show that there is *no* such proposition, it suggests that finding one is much more difficult than most atheologians seem to suppose."[4] Now while Plantinga cannot be faulted for not exploring the entire range of propositions essential to theism, since after all the range is quite enormous, it would seem that he restricted his scope of examination unduly because he thinks that (e) itself is the only likely candidate for the proposition that is both essential to theism and relevant to the deduction of the denial of (g). Plantinga does not say why he thinks that (e) is the only likely candidate out of the enormous number of contenders and I think that he rejects even this candidate too swiftly because it is not at all clear that his claim that (i) entails (k)[5] is correct, and if it is not then he himself has produced a plausible candidate for the proposition which will permit the deduction of the denial of (g). However, I do not want to argue this point. What I want to show is that there are other candidates. I want to show that there are three other propositions, and perhaps there are more for all I know, which are essential to theism and which jointly entail the *denial* of (g) such that when they are added to (a)–(e) and (f₄) the result is a set of propositions which entails the contradictory conjunction of (g) and the denial of (g).

It is quite plain that (a)–(e) does not even approach the limit of exhausting the possible list of propositions essential to orthodox theism. Furthermore, it would seem that

(1) God exists and created everything *ex nihilo* and in time

is a proposition essential to theism and that (1) entails both

(2) Prior to creation there was nothing but God

and

(3) Subsequent to creation there is nothing which is not casually dependent upon God,

but the conjunction of (2) and (3) entails

(4) If God had not created there would be nothing but God;

and since another proposition essential to orthodox theism is that

(5) God is the greatest possible good,

then the theist is committed to the proposition that

(6) If God had not created there would be nothing but the greatest possible good,

because (4) and (5) jointly entail (6). Now since the theist also holds that God is wholly free it would seem that the theist is also committed to the proposition that

(7) God need not have created;

but then (6) and (7) entail

(8) The existence of the greatest possible good does not entail the existence of any other thing;

and (8) entails

(9) The existence of the greatest possible good does not entail the existence of any evil state of affairs.

From (9) it would seem to follow that

(10) Every evil state of affairs is such that for every good that entails it, there is a greater good that does not;

and from (10) it follows that

(11) If there is any evil, then for every good that entails it, there is a greater good that does not.

Now the conjunction of (e), that evil exists, and (11) entails

(12) There is at least one evil state of affairs such that for every good
that entails it, there is a greater good that does not;

and since (12) is the denial of (g) and (g) is entailed by the conjunction
of (a)–(e) and (f_4), the conjunction of (a)–(e) and (f_4) together with (1),
(5), and (7) constitutes a set of propositions, let us call it *S,* which entails
the contradictory conjunction of (g) and the denial of (g). So, it would
appear that the atheologian can, contrary to what Plantinga believes, identify a set of propositions, (1), (5), and (7), which are essential to theism
and entail the denial of (g) such that when these new propositions are
added to the others they produce the set *S* which entails a contradiction.

But even so, Plantinga would reject the claim that *S* shows that theism
is inconsistent and that evil is unjustified because he finds a further difficulty
with (f_4). It seems quite clear that (f_4) entails

(F) An omnipotent, omniscient person who is wholly good can permit
an evil state of affairs to exist only if it is entailed by a good
which outweighs it.

Now if (F) is false then (f_4) is false and the theist can reject (f_4) and escape
the charge of inconsistency because *S* would not then show that theism
is self-contradictory or that evil is unjustified, and in chapter 6 of *God
and Other Minds* Plantinga says that (F) is by no means self-evident and
that apologists for traditional theism have often denied it.[6] These apologists,
then, attempt to escape the charge of inconsistency in their theistic belief
by claiming that (F) is false. They sustain their claim that an omnipotent,
omniscient person can permit evil which is not entailed by some good
without forfeiting His claim to moral goodness by arguing that perhaps
there are certain good states of affairs that an omnipotent God *cannot*
bring about without permitting evil, even though these do not entail any
evil at all. An omnipotent God, for example, cannot bring about free
will and its attendant moral goods without also bringing about the possibility of evil, even though these goods do not entail any evil. This position,
according to Plantinga, is sometimes called the free will defense. The free
will argument is an argument intended to sustain the theist's claim that
(F) is false and to provide an escape from the charge of inconsistency.

But the free will argument does not get the theist off the hook. While
it *may* be adequate to sustain the claim that (F) is false, the free will
argument has as one of its essential premises that God is not morally
culpable for the evil in the world because God could prevent moral evil

only by preventing the possibility of moral good which outweighs it. In Plantinga's formulation of the free will argument he states this premise by saying: "The fact that free creatures sometimes err, however, in no way tells against God's omnipotence or against His goodness; for He could forestall the occurrence of moral evil only by removing the possibility of moral good."[7] In other words, God escapes the charge of moral culpability because preventing evil *entails* preventing the possibility of moral good which outweighs it. So while the theist denies (f_4) he is presumably committed to the claim that

(f_4') An omnipotent, omniscient person is wholly good only if he prevents every evil E which is such that preventing E does not entail
preventing the possibility of moral good which outweighs E

and it would seem, then, that we could say that an evil state of affairs is *justified* just in case it is false that preventing it does not entail preventing the possibility of moral good which outweighs it.

Now while (a)–(e) and (f_4) do not entail the denial of (e), they do jointly entail

(g') Every evil E is such that preventing E entails preventing the
possibility of moral good which outweighs E.

So the atheologian can still convict the theist of inconsistency and show that evil is unjustified if he can find a set of propositions which is such that each member of the set is either necessarily true, or essential to theism, or a logical consequence of such propositions and which is such that the entire set entails the denial of (g'):

There is at least one evil state of affairs such that preventing it does not entail preventing the possibility of moral good which outweighs it.

The issue, then, is whether or not the atheologian can find a set of propositions which satisfy these conditions. I think that he can and it is not necessary to go very far beyond the set of propositions (1)–(12) in order to produce a set satisfying these conditions.

Since the theist believes not only that God is the greatest possible good but also that His goodness is the highest moral goodness, it would seem that a further claim essential to theism is the claim that

(13) The greatest possible good is moral good which outweighs any possible evil,

and that the theist is committed to the proposition that

(14) If God had not created there would exist moral good which outweighs any possible evil

because (6), from (1)–(12), and (13) jointly entail (14). Furthermore, (4) from (1)–(12) entails

(15) If God had not created there would be no evil;

and (15) together with (7) from (1)–(12) entails

(16) God could prevent evil by not creating.

Now from the conjunction of (14) and (16) it follows that

(17) God could prevent evil without preventing the existence of moral good which outweighs it;

and since it would seem to be necessarily true that

(18) What is actual is possible,

then it would seem that the theist is committed to the proposition that

(19) God could prevent evil without preventing the possibility of moral good which outweighs it,

because (19) follows from the conjunction of (17) and (18). But (19) entails

(20) Every evil state of affairs is such that preventing it does not entail preventing the possibility of moral good which outweighs it;

and from (20) it follows that

(21) If there is any evil then preventing it does not entail preventing the possibility of moral good which outweighs it.

Now the conjunction of (e), that evil exists, and (21) entails

(22) There is at least one evil state of affairs such that preventing it does not entail preventing the possibility of moral good which outweighs it;

and since (22) is the denial of (g′) and (g′) is entailed by the conjunction of (a)–(e) and (f₄′), the conjunction (a)–(e) and (f₄′) together with (1), (5),

(7), (13), and (18) constitutes a set of propositions—let us call it S'—which entails the contradictory conjunction of (g') and the denial of (g'). So, it would appear that the atheologian can identify a set of propositions which are either necessarily true or essential to theism and which entail the denial of (g') such that when these new propositions are added to the others they produce the set S' which both entails a contradiction and which is such that each member of S' is either necessarily true, or essential to theism, or a logical consequence of such propositions. In short, while S may not show that theism is inconsistent or that evil is unjustified, the atheologian can produce S' to convict the theist of inconsistency and to show that evil is unjustified.

Furthermore, since (20) says that every evil state of affairs is such that preventing it does not entail preventing the possibility of moral good which outweighs it, then (20) and (f_4') entail that if there is an omnipotent, omniscient person who is wholly good then he prevents every evil. But (a)–(e) asserts that there is such a person. So, (a)–(e) and (f_4') together with (20) entail that there is no evil, that is, they entail the denial of (e). Not only does S' entail (g') and the denial of (g'), S' also entails both (e) and the denial of (e).

It is not at all clear how Plantinga would answer the preceding argument because his ingenious proofs in Chapter Six are devoted to a defense of the free will argument against certain specific attacks, and since the preceding argument does not challenge the free will argument Plantinga's proofs do not speak against it. What the preceding argument shows is that the issue about evil, which the free will argument raises between the theist and the atheologian, is one which really misses the main problem for theism because this issue is usually discussed in such a way as to suggest that God had only two choices with respect to creation, either to create a world with evil or to create a world without evil. The atheologian usually assumes that the theist has a problem just in case God could have created differently, that is, just in case God could have created a world without evil. The theist then counters that there is no problem because, after all, God could not have created differently, that is, God could not have created a world without evil or at least the possibility of evil which as a matter of fact became actualized.

But the question of whether or not God could have created a world without evil misses the point because it is false that theism has a problem *just in case* God could have created differently: the theist has a problem even if God could not have created differently. What the preceding argument shows is that if the theist is right in some of his claims about God, then God is the creator and a wholly free being who did not have just the options of either creating a world with evil or creating a world without evil: He had the further choice of not creating at all. No matter what is accepted about what God could or could not do with a creation, or what God ought or ought not to have done with a creation, it remains that the beliefs of orthodox theism entail both that God need not have created and that if God had not created then there would be no evil at all. On the theist's own view, then, in order to prevent evil God need not have created in a special way. He could have failed to create altogether and without any loss of free will or moral goodness because the theist also holds that God is wholly free and the highest moral good. Perhaps God could not, for some perfectly plausible reason, create a world without evil, but then it would seem that He ought not to have created at all. If the theist is right in some of his claims about God and evil, then being omniscient and prior to creation God knew that if He created there would be evil, so being wholly good He ought not to have created.

In order to escape this argument what the theist needs is an apologetic of creation and such an apologetic, it would seem, must come into conflict with at least one of the theist's other claims about God because on the theist's own view prior to creation there was nothing missing from the perfect value of God which would call for creation. One possible approach to a satisfactory apologetic of creation, for example, might be to point out that if God had not created then there would be no *human* free will or *human* moral good. But this kind of an approach would require a further premise to the effect that a created hierarchy of value adds to the overall value and, hence, God created. It would follow from this, however, that created value adds to God's value and, hence, that God is not the greatest possible good because His godness can be increased by the addition of created value. So this approach would not appear to be very promising nor, would it appear, is any other kind of approach because such an apologetic would have to state that God had to create for some reason or other and this would seem to be in direct conflict either with the view that God is wholly free or the view that God has no motives, such as needs or wants, which would adequately explain the alleged creative act. So it would appear that theism is inconsistent and that the theist must give up one or more of his claims about God.

NOTES

1. Alvin Plantinga, *God and Other Minds* (Ithaca, N.Y.: Cornell University Press, 1967), pp. 115-30.

2. Plantinga makes it clear on p. 120 that, to say that one state of affairs entails another state of affairs, is to say that the proposition that the one obtains, entails the proposition that the other obtains.

3. Ibid., p. 122.

4. Ibid., p. 128.

5. See p. 125 for Plantinga's discussion of (i) and (k).

6. Ibid., p. 131.

7. Ibid., p. 132.

5

God Might Not Love Us

In a carefully reasoned article[1] James Tomberlin presented a critical study of Alvin Plantinga's *God and Other Minds*.[2] In this study Tomberlin finds, among other things, a major difficulty with Plantinga's account of God's immutability.[3] Tomberlin argues that on Plantinga's account of God's immutability it turns out that the common doctrine that God is omniscient is *logically inconsistent* with the view that God has all of His nonrelational properties essentially. However, in a subsequent critique of this argument[4] Tomberlin provides a solution to the difficulty. There he argues that the logical inconsistency results from a deficiency in Plantinga's formulation of the distinction between relational and nonrelational properties and he provides a version of this distinction which has the result that the doctrine that God is omniscient is *not* logically inconsistent with the view that God has all of His nonrelational properties essentially.

Given Tomberlin's solution, then, one might be tempted to conclude that the theist is better off rejecting Plantinga's formulation of the distinction between relational and nonrelational properties in favor of Tomberlin's formulation. But while Tomberlin's formulation of this distinction does not yield the undesirable results that Plantinga's formulation does, Tomberlin's version suffers a different but equally serious difficulty and it too must be rejected by the theist. The difficulty is that Tomberlin's formulation of the distinction between relational and nonrelational properties

From *International Journal for Philosophy of Religion* 5, no. 3 (Fall 1974): 57–61. Reprinted by permission.

is *logically inconsistent* with the pre-analytical claim of orthodox theism that the property of loving everyone is among the properties which God has in some necessary manner. In order to show how this inconsistency arises let us summarize both Plantinga's accounts of God's immutability as well as Tomberlin's criticism and solution of this account.

In the section in question of *God and Other Minds*[5] Plantinga's general program is to explicate the view that God possesses His various properties in some necessary manner and more explicitly, for example, to explicate the claim that God possesses in some necessary manner the properties of loving everyone, being omniscient, and being everlasting. Plantinga's account involves explaining relational properties, nonrelational properties, and essential properties which he does as follows:

(P1) God has *P relationally* if and only if the proposition that God has *P* entails the existence of some contingent being distinct from God.

(P2) God has *P nonrelationally* if and only if God has *P,* but He does not have *P* relationally (in the sense of [P1])

(P3) God has *P essentially* if and only if the proposition that God lacks *P* is necessarily false.

Now according to Plantinga, the claim that God possesses His various properties in some necessary manner entails, at the very least, the absence of certain kinds of *change* in God, that is, it entails that God is *changeless.* Furthermore, Plantinga points out, a being undergoes change just in case it possesses at one time a property that it lacks at another time. But with this understanding of change it is quite clear that God *does* undergo change because, for example, the property of being worshiped by St. Paul is a property which God possessed in A.D. 40 but lacked in 100 B.C. Under these circumstances, then, how are we to understand the claim that God is changeless and, hence, understand the claim that God possesses His various properties in some necessary manner where these properties presumably include the properties of loving everyone, being omniscient, and being everlasting?

Plantinga explicates the claim that God is changeless by appealing to the definitions (P1)–(P3). By (P1) and (P2) God has both relational and nonrelational properties. Plantinga points out, for example, that the property of being worshiped by St. Paul would be one of God's relational properties whereas the properties of loving everyone, being omniscient, and being everlasting are among God's nonrelational properties. In accordance with (P1), then, Plantinga suggests that to say that God is *changeless* is to say that

(P4) Any property that God has at one time but lacks at another is one of His relational properties.

Furthermore, another way of understanding the claim that God is *changeless* is to say that God is changeless with respect to His nonrelational properties. In accordance with (P2), then, Plantinga suggests that to say that God is *changeless* is to say that

(P5) All of God's nonrelational properties are properties that He *cannot* fail to have.

In addition, the claim of (P5) can be put more precisely by stating that claim in terms of St. Augustine's distinction between essential and accidental properties. If we construe St. Augustine's distinction in terms of Plantinga's definition in (P3) then to say that God is *changeless* is to say that

(P6) God has all His nonrelational properties essentially (in the sense of [P3]).

It turns out, then, that Plantinga's account of God's immutability is *logically consistent* with the pre-analytical claim of orthodox theism that the properties of loving everyone, being omniscient, and being everlasting are properties that God has in some necessary manner. By (P2) these properties are nonrelational properties and by (P6) they are properties that God has essentially, that is, they are properties that God cannot fail to have.

Nevertheless, Tomberlin points out[6] that *there is a logical inconsistency* between the common doctrine that God is omniscient and the claim of (P6) that God has *all* His nonrelational properties essentially because by God's omniscience He has the property of knowing there are no unicorns. So, Tomberlin argues, from (P1) and (P2) it follows that God has this property nonrelationally, since His having it does not entail the existence of any contingent being distinct from Himself. But God cannot have this property essentially because the proposition "If there are unicorns, God does not know there are no unicorns" is necessarily true and the proposition "There are unicorns" is possibly true. So, it is possible that God does not know there are no unicorns, but then by (P3) if God is omniscient He cannot have as an essential property the nonrelational property of knowing there are no unicorns. It turns out, then, that the doctrine that

God is omniscient is logically inconsistent with the doctrine that God has all of His nonrelational properties essentially and that the theist must either abandon one of these doctrines or abandon (P1)–(P3) as an explication of the latter doctrine.

Now Tomberlin suggests that the source of the difficulty is (P1) because the property of knowing there are no unicorns turns out to be nonrelational for God by (P1) while it should be construed as relational since it is a property God might not have had. Accordingly, Tomberlin proposes that the theist abandon (P1) and that instead we distinguish God's relational properties from His nonrelational properties as follows:

(T1)   God has *P relationally* if and only if (either *God has P* or *God has not-P* entails the existence of some contingent being distinct from God) or (either *God has P* or *God has not-P* entails *God has Q*, where *Q* is not identical with either *P* or *not-P*, and *God has Q* entails the existence of some contingent being distinct from God),

adding that God has *P* nonrelationally just in case He has *P* but not relationally (in the sense of [T1]). By (T1), then, the property of knowing there are no unicorns will be one of God's relational properties and there will be no logical inconsistency in holding both that God is omniscient and that God has all of His nonrelational properties essentially. So, according to Tomberlin, the difficulty is removed for the theist if he rejects (P1) in favor of (T1) because (T1) explains "God has *P* relationally" in such a way that His relational properties are all and only those properties He might not have had.

But Tomberlin is mistaken in thinking that the theist is better off with (T1) than he is with (P1) and we are now in a position to see why. According to the pre-analytical claims of traditional theism the property of loving everyone is a property which God has in some necessary manner. Put in terms of the present discussion the claim that God has this property in some necessary manner is the claim, consistent with (P1), that *the property of loving everyone is a nonrelational property of God which He cannot fail to have.* But now notice that the proposition

(1) God has the property of not loving everyone

entails

(2) God has the property of being such that there is at least one person God does not love

where the property of being such that there is at least one person God does not love is not identical to either the property of loving everyone or the property of not loving everyone. Furthermore, notice that (2) entails the existence of a contingent being distinct from God. But then from (T1) it follows that the property of loving everyone is a relational property and being a relational property it is a property that God might not have had. Indeed, being a property that God might not have had, the property of loving everyone might very well be, for all we know, a property that God does not have. By (T1), for all we know, God might *not* love us.

The result, it would appear, is that the theist is no better off with Tomberlin's formulation of the distinction between relational and non-relational properties than he is with Plantinga's formulation. Tomberlin's formulation is logically inconsistent with the view that loving everyone is a nonrelational property of God that He *cannot* fail to have and if the theist is to be consistent in his views he must either abandon that view or reject (T1).

NOTES

1. "Plantinga's Puzzles About God and Other Minds," *The Philosophical Forum* 1, no. 3 (Spring 1969, New Series): 365–91.

2. Alvin Plantinga, *God and Other Minds* (Ithaca, N.Y.: Cornell University Press, 1967).

3. Tomberlin's critique of this account occurs in pages 376–84 of his study.

4. "Omniscience and Necessity: Putting Humpty-Dumpty Together Again," *The Philosophical Forum* 2, no. 1 (Fall 1970, New Series): 149–51.

5. For a full account see pages 173–83 of Plantinga's *God and Other Minds*.

6. In "Omniscience and Necessity" Tomberlin provides a summary of his original criticism in addition to his proposed solution.

6

Swinburne on Omnipotence

Adopting the principle that any definition of omnipotence must be rejected which entails either (a) that an omnipotent being can bring about a state of affairs which it is logically impossible for him to bring about or (b) that a being clearly not omnipotent is omnipotent, Richard Swinburne[1] claims to have provided a successful definition of omnipotence. What Swinburne accepts as a successful definition is the fifth and last formulation in a series of provisional formulations which he considers for analysis and criticism. Except for the first formulation which is posited as the one that initially suggests itself, each succeeding formulation in the series is presented as a solution to certain problems which befall the formulation immediately preceding it in the series and which are posed as problems by recent criticisms of the coherence of the concept of omnipotence cited by Swinburne. The success Swinburne sees for the last formulation consists in the fact that it is immune to the problems posed by these recent criticisms. But while Swinburne's definition does indeed overcome all the recent criticisms of the coherence of the concept of omnipotence which he cites, and even one such criticism that he does not cite,[2] and while his definition does not seem to entail either (a) or (b) above, the definition suffers a different but equally fatal flaw. I will show that Swinburne's definition of omnipotence is *not* successful if it is to be counted as a mark of the success of a definition of omnipotence that the definition be logically consistent with the other

From *International Journal for Philosophy of Religion* 6, no. 4 (Winter 1975): 251–55. Reprinted by permission.

doctrines essential to traditional Judaeo-Christian theism. I will argue that Swinburne's definition of omnipotence is logically incompatible with the doctrine of divine omniscience and, hence, that no traditional theist can accept his definition and consistently maintain that God is *both* omnipotent *and* omniscient.

The following sentence and list of provisions constitutes what Swinburne offers as his successful definition of omnipotence.

[E] ($\forall S$) ($\forall t$) [(S is omnipotent at t) $\equiv_L$ ($\forall x$) { (x is a logically contingent state of affairs after t) & (The occurrence of x after t does not entail that S did not bring about x at t) $\rightarrow$ (S is able at t to bring about x) }] provided that:

(i) 'S' ranges over all existent beings.

(ii) 'x' ranges over all logically possible states of affairs.

(iii) The 'L' adjoined to the equivalence sign indicates that the equivalence is logical, not material.

(iv) The '$\rightarrow$' is the sign of material implication.

(v) By "x is a logically contingent state of affairs" is meant "both x and not-x are logically possible states of affairs" and we must understand here by x being a logically possible state of affairs after t that x be not merely logically possible and after t but that x be a state of affairs logically compatible with what has happened at and before t.

(vi) The assertion (i) that the range of 'S' is all existent beings is to be understood only as saying that [E] licenses any formula obtained by substituting in it for 'S' the *proper name* of any existing being. We cannot substitute for 'S' a definite description.

Formulation [D], the predecessor of [E], did not include the condition of [E] that the occurrence of x after t does not entail that S did not bring about x at t. Consequently, [D] entailed that in order for S to be omnipotent in 1973, S must be able to bring about a state of affairs in 1974 not brought about by S because the state of affairs in question is logically contingent after 1973. But since an omnipotent being cannot be expected to bring about a state of affairs which it is logically impossible for him to bring about, Swinburne rejected [D] in favor of [E] which does not appear to entail this difficulty. Furthermore, [D] did not include provision (vi) which limits the substituend set of the variable "S" in [E] *to only* proper names. Swinburne added this provision to [E] in order to overcome a difficulty mentioned by Alvin Plantinga[3] in connection with another definition of omnipotence. Without provision (vi) we could substitute for "*S*" in [E] the definite description "the man who is capable only of scratching his ear." Definition [E], then, would entail that the man who is capable only of scratching his ear is omnipotent, if he exists. This is so because such a man would be able to bring about at *t* any logically contingent state of affairs whose occurrence after *t* does not entail that the man who is capable only of scratching his ear did not bring it about at *t*. For the only states of affairs whose occurrences after *t* do *not* entail that the man in question did not bring them about at *t* are the scratchings of the ear of the man in question. So, the occurrence after *t* of *any other* state of affairs, the shooting of a rifle, for example, entails that the man who is capable only of scratching his ear did not bring that state of affairs about at *t*. Without provision (vi), then, [E] entails that if there is a man who is capable only of scratching his ear then such a man is omnipotent. With provision (vi), [E] would appear to be immune to this difficulty.

But consider now Mr. McEar. Mr. McEar is the man who is capable only of scratching his ear. That is, "McEar" is the proper name of the man who has the property of being able only to scratch his ear. Someone might want to argue that despite provision (vi) definition [E] entails that McEar is omnipotent if he exists. It might be argued that except for the scratchings of his ear, the occurrence after *t* of *any other* state of affairs entails that McEar did not bring about that state of affairs at *t* because McEar *is* the man who is capable only of scratching his ear. Though Swinburne did not consider this possible objection, it is fairly clear what form of response would be required to overcome it. The proper response is that while the occurrence after *t* of just *any* state of affairs other than the scratching of his ear entails directly, without the aid of additional claims, that the man who is capable only of scratching his ear did not bring about that state of affairs at *t,* the same does not hold for McEar. The occurrence after *t* of just *any* state of affairs other than the scratching of his ear does *not* entail that McEar did not bring about that state of affairs at *t* unless it is *added* that McEar is the man who is capable only of scratching his ear. But since provision (vi) allows only for the substitution of proper names for "*S*" in [E] and not for the addition of further claims about *S,* [E] does not entail that McEar is omnipotent even though McEar is the man who is capable only of scratching his ear. Accordingly,

this possible objection does no damage to Swinburne's definition of omnipotence.

Nevertheless, there is a problem with the definition. Consider the state
of affairs, call it A, which has the property of having been brought about
by a being who never at any time has the property of being omniscient.
Now, it would appear that [E] entails that in order for S to be omnipotent
in 1974, S must be able to bring about A in 1974. But, then, the *ability*
of S in 1974 to bring about A in 1974 entails that S is not omniscient
because it entails that S never at any time has the property of being
omniscient. So, since Swinburne's definition of omnipotence holds for all
existent beings, the definition entails that if any being is omnipotent then
it is not omniscient. It follows, then, that God is not omniscient, if He
is omnipotent.

In order to avoid this consequence it would seem that we must either
deny that A is a logically contingent state of affairs after 1974 or say
that the occurrence of A after 1974 entails that S did not bring about
A in 1974. But it is hard to see how either of these alternative defenses
could be sustained, even if we substitute the proper name "God" for "S."
Assuming that substitution, the first defense could be sustained only if
it is false that both A and not-A are logically possible states of affairs
or if something happened in or before 1974 that is logically incompatible
with A. But both A and not-A would seem to be logically possible states
of affairs and I myself do not know of anything that happened in or
before 1974 that is logically incompatible with a state of affairs which
has the property of having been brought about by a being who never
at any time has the property of being omniscient.

On the other hand, the second defense that the occurrence of A after
1974 entails that God did not bring A about in 1974 could be sustained
only if we add the claim that God is omniscient. For clearly the occurrence
in 1975 of a state of affairs which has the property of having been brought
about by a being who never at any time has the property of being omniscient
does not entail that the being named by the proper name "God" did not
bring that state of affairs about in 1974 *unless* we also add the further
claim that the being named by the proper name "God" is the being who
is omniscient. But, as we have already seen in connection with the discussion
of Mr. McEar, provision (vi) does not allow for adding such claims as
"Mr. McEar is the man who is capable only of scratching his ear" or
"God is omniscient." In any case, it would appear that any further provision
added to [E] which would allow us to say that the occurrence of A after

1974 entails that God did not bring *A* about in 1974 would also allow us to say that the occurrence after *t* of *any* state of affairs other than the scratching of his ear entails that McEar did not bring about the state of affairs at *t*. But, then, any such provision of [E] that would allow these things would have the result that [E] entails that Mr. McEar is omnipotent if he exists. So, it would appear that no further provisions can be added to definition [E] to avoid the consequence of that definition that if God is omnipotent then He is not omniscient. What is needed here is a complete modification and reformulation of [E] which results in a definition of omnipotence that does *not* entail either that McEar is omnipotent or that God is not omniscient. How this is to be accomplished is a problem for which I have no present solution.

It turns out, then, that while Swinburne has achieved what appears to be a coherent definition of divine omnipotence, the coherence of the definition is paid for by sacrificing divine omniscience. So, because his definition of omnipotence is logically incompatible with the doctrine of divine omniscience, no theist can consistently maintain that God is *both* omnipotent *and* omniscient and accept Swinburne's definition as well.

NOTES

1. Richard Swinburne, "Omnipotence," *American Philosophical Quarterly* 10, no. 3 (July 1973): 231–37.

2. James Cargile, "On Omnipotence," *Nous* 1 (May 1967): 201–205. Considering the possibility that 'God is omnipotent' means 'God can create any state of affairs S such that *God creates S* is consistent,' Cargile points out that the definition entails *both* that God can bring about a state of affairs in which there exists a chicken which has the property of having been created by a being which has never at any time had the power to create a duck *and* that God can bring about a state of affairs in which there exists a duck which has the property of having been created by a being which has never at any time had the power to create a chicken. Swinburne's definition is free from this entailment.

3. Alvin Plantinga, *God and Other Minds* (Ithaca, N.Y.: Cornell University Press, 1967), p. 170.

7

Aquinas on the Self-Evidence of God's Existence

In the *Summa Theologia* I (STI), beginning at question 2, article 3, and in the *Summa Contra Gentiles* I (CGI), beginning at chapter 13, Aquinas provides five proofs for the existence of God. These proofs are intended to *demonstrate* that God exists and to provide the foundation for a larger program to *demonstrate* many other doctrines which are held by faith. However, the program which Aquinas sets up for himself in the two great *Summae* is trivial and unnecessary if the existence of God is self-evident in such a way that God's existence needs no demonstration. So, as a preamble to the five ways, Aquinas argues that the existence of God is not self-evident in any way that would hinder his program of rational theology.

In STI the argument occurs in question 2, article 1, and in CGI it occurs in chapters 10 and 11. Aquinas also argues the same point in *Commentum in Primum Librum Sententiarum* (CS) distinction 3, question 1, article 2, and in *Quaestiones Disputate De Veritate* (DV) question 10, article 12. In addition, Aquinas makes further relevant remarks on this point both in other passages in the works already cited and in other works, most notably *Quaestiones Disputate De Potentia* question 7, article 2, and in *In Libros Posteriorum Analyticorum Expositio* I lectures 10 through 15. What I will be concerned with in this discussion is to show that Aquinas' arguments fail. I will not argue that God's existence is in any way self-evident, but only that the account which Aquinas gives of his thesis about the self-

From *Canadian Journal of Philosophy* 6, no. 3 (1976): 443–54. Reprinted by permission.

evidence of God's existence does not foreclose the possibility of holding that God's existence is self-evident in such a way as to hinder his program.

The thesis for which Aquinas argues in STI, CGI, CS, and DV is that while the proposition 'God exists' is a self-evident (*per se nota*) proposition, it is not self-evident in such a way that we can know *that* God exists simply by virtue of the fact that the proposition is self-evident in that way, and we cannot know (aside from faith) *that* God exists without a demonstration *quia;* that is, we cannot know *that* God exists unless the proposition 'God exists' occurs as the conclusion of a proof which argues from God's effects to His existence as a cause. Aquinas begins his argument for this thesis by distinguishing two ways in which a proposition can be self-evident. According to Aquinas either

1. a proposition is self-evident in itself and not self-evident to us (i.e., self-evident to none of us), or

2. a proposition is self-evident in itself and self-evident to us (i.e., self-evident to some of us or all of us).

Now presumably a proposition which is self-evident in the first way is a proposition which *cannot* be known by us to be true simply by virtue of the fact that it is self-evident in that way, while a proposition which is self-evident in the second way is a proposition which *can* be known by us to be true simply by virtue of the fact that it is self-evident in that way. So, on the basis of this distinction Aquinas defends his thesis by arguing that the proposition 'God exists' is self-evident in the first way but not self-evident in the second way. His argument consists in explicating the difference between these two ways of being self-evident and attempting to show that the proposition 'God exists' does not satisfy the conditions of the second, crucial, way of being self-evident.

For the purpose of explicating the difference between his two ways of being self-evident Aquinas states the condition under which a proposition is self-evident *in itself* (*in se*). Though he formulates it differently in each passage the statement of this condition can be expressed by saying that

(S) a proposition is self-evident *in itself* when the predicate of the proposition is included in the meaning or nature (*ratio*) of the subject.

In CGI, chapter 11, Aquinas refers to propositions which satisfy the condition in (S) as propositions which are self-evident *simpliciter*. As examples of propositions which he thinks are self-evident *simpliciter* Aquinas mentions at one time or another in these passages the following propositions:

(a) Man is an animal (STI, CGI, and CS).

(b) Every whole is greater than one of its parts (STI, CGI, DV, and CS).

(c) Equal quantities subtracted from equal things yields equal things having equal quantities (DV).

(d) Affirmation and negation cannot be simultaneously true (STl and DV).

(e) Incorporeal things do not occupy space (STI and DV).

(f) God exists (STI, CGI, DV, and CS).

According to Aquinas each of these propositions is one in which the predicate is included in the meaning or nature of the subject and, hence, by (S) each one is a proposition which is self-evident *simpliciter*.

Now, since for Aquinas the state of affairs of satisfying the condition in (S) is a state of affairs which obtains independently of any human activity, being self-evident *simpliciter* is a property possessed by propositions independently of any human activity. So, it is clearly possible on Aquinas' view for a proposition to satisfy both the condition that it has the property of being self-evident *simpliciter* and the condition that no one knows that it has the property of being self-evident *simpliciter*. Let us call this set of conditions C1. Indeed, there may be many propositions which are self-evident *simpliciter* and which no one knows to be self-evident *simpliciter*. Furthermore, since for Aquinas it is possible to know for some propositions that the predicate is included in the meaning or nature of the subject, it is possible to know for some propositions that they have the property of being self-evident *simpliciter*. So, it is clearly possible on Aquinas' view for a proposition to satisfy both the condition that it has the property of being self-evident *simpliciter* and the condition that we know that it has the property of being self-evident *simpliciter*. Let us call this set of conditions C2. Indeed, there are many propositions which are self-evident *simpliciter* and which are known to be self-evident *simpliciter*. Accordingly, we might suppose that if there are any propositions satisfying the set of conditions C1, then they are self-evident in Aquinas' first way and that any proposition satisfying the set of conditions C2 is self-evident in Aquinas' second way. That is, we might possibly expect that Aquinas would explicate the difference between his two ways of being self-evident in terms of whether or not a proposition is known by us to be self-evident *simpliciter*. We might have thought, perhaps, that Aquinas would explicate 1 and 2 by saying something like the following:

1.1 a proposition P is self-evident in itself and *not* self-evident to us if P is self-evident *simpliciter* and no one knows that P is self-evident *simpliciter* (i.e., if the predicate of P is included in the *meaning* or nature of the subject of P and no one knows *that* the predicate of P is included in the meaning or nature of the subject of P), and

2.1 a proposition P is self-evident in itself and self-evident to *us* if P is self-evident *simpliciter* and we know *that* P is self-evident *simpliciter* (i.e., if the predicate of P is included in the meaning or nature of the subject of P and we know *that* the predicate of P is included in the meaning or nature of the subject of P).

But Aquinas does not explicate the difference between his two ways of being self-evident in these terms. Even though he recognizes that it is possible for a proposition to satisfy the set of conditions C1 or the set of conditions C2, Aquinas does not analyze the difference between 1 and 2 in terms of whether or not we *know that* a proposition is self-evident *simpliciter*. On Aquinas' view it is possible for a proposition to satisfy the set of conditions C2 and yet not be self-evident to us. In fact, for Aquinas the proposition in (f), 'God exists,' is an example of such a proposition. Aquinas claims to know that

(g) essence and existence are *identical* in God

and, hence, by (S), to know that (f) is self-evident *simpliciter* because by (g) the predicate of (f) is included in the meaning or nature of the subject of (f). Furthermore, he holds that (f) is *not* self-evident to us. So, on Aquinas' view the proposition 'God exists' is self-evident *simpliciter* and he knows that it is self-evident *simpliciter,* but it is not self-evident to us; that is, it is not self-evident in such a way that we can know that it is true simply by virtue of the fact that it is self-evident in that way. But by (S) and 2.1 (f) would be both self-evident *simpliciter* and self-evident to us if we know that (g) obtains. Consequently, Aquinas' stand on (S), (g), and (f) will not permit him to subscribe to 1.1 and 2.1 as an explication of his two ways of being self-evident.

Instead, Aquinas explicates the difference between his two ways of being self-evident in terms of whether or not we know the meaning or nature of the subject and predicate of a proposition which is self-evident *simpliciter.* Though he formulates it differently in each passage Aquinas' explication of 1 and 2 can be expressed by saying:

1.2 a proposition P is self-evident in itself and *not* self-evident to us if and only if P is self-evident *simpliciter* and no one knows the meaning or nature of the subject *or* predicate of P (i.e., if and only if the predicate of P is included in the meaning or nature of the subject of P and no one knows the meaning or nature of the subject *or* predicate of P), and

2.2 a proposition P is self-evident in itself and self-evident *to us* if and only if P is self-evident *simpliciter* and we know the meaning or nature of the subject *and* predicate of P (i.e., if and only if the predicate of P is included in the meaning or nature of the subject of P and we know the meaning or nature of the subject *and* predicate of P).

On the basis of this explication of his distinction Aquinas completes the defense of his thesis by pointing out that unlike the propositions in (a) through (e), the proposition in (f), 'God exists,' does not satisfy the condition in 2.2. Aquinas maintains that the propositions in (a) through (d) are self-evident to everyone because "they contain common kinds of terms about which no one is ignorant" (*quorum termini sunt quaedam communia quae nullus ignorat* STI 2, 1) while the proposition in (e) is self-evident only to the learned "because the ability of untrained people to understand does not go beyond the ability to understand the content of mental images, so they are unable to achieve an understanding of the meaning or nature of incorporeal bodies" (*quia scilicet vulgi consideratio imaginationem transcendere non potest, ut ad rationem rei incorporalis pertingat* DV 10, 12). On the other hand, Aquinas maintains that because the proposition in (f) satisfies the condition in (S) the proposition is self-evident *simpliciter,* but "because we do not know what God is the proposition is not self-evident to us" (*quia nos non scimus de Deo quid est non est nobis per se nota* STI 2, 1); that is, "because the essence of God is not known by us it is not self-evident to us that God exists" (*quia quidditas Dei non est nobis nota, ideo quo ad nos Deum esse non est per se notum* DV 10, 12). Therefore, according to Aquinas, the proposition 'God exists' is self-evident *simpliciter,* but it is not self-evident by the condition of 2.2; that is, it is not self-evident in such a way that we can know that the proposition is true simply by virtue of the fact that it is self-evident in that way. To know that the proposition is true, aside from faith, we need a demonstration for it.

By virtue of Aquinas' explication, then, if the condition obtains that we know the meaning or nature of the subject and predicate of a proposition which is self-evident *simpliciter* then the proposition is self-evident to us and that that condition obtains is not only sufficient but also necessary in order for the proposition to be self-evident to us. So, on Aquinas' view, given any proposition which is self-evident *simpliciter*, each proposition in (a) through (f) for example, the issue of whether or not the proposition is self-evident to us can be settled by determining whether it satisfies the condition in 1.2 or the condition in 2.2, that is, by determining whether or not we know the meaning or nature of the subject and predicate of the proposition.

But now the difficulty with Aquinas' defense is that while it may be true that we *do not* know the meaning or nature of the subject of the proposition in (f) and that we *do* know the meaning or nature of the subjects and predicates of the propositions in (a) through (e), it is not at all clear that we can ever actually determine whether or not we know these things. The reason for this is that it is not at all clear that on Aquinas' view we can ever actually determine whether or not we know the meaning or nature of the subject and predicate of *any* proposition which is self-evident *simpliciter*. Aquinas tells us that the proposition in (f), 'God exists,' does not satisfy the condition that we know the meaning or nature of the subject of the proposition because we do not know the *quid est* or *quidditas* of God. But it would appear to be the case that on Aquinas' view the essential feature of knowing the *quidditas* of a subject is that knowing the *quidditas* of a subject entails and is entailed by knowing *all* of the essential properties of that subject. So, since a statement to the effect that an essential property of a subject actually belongs to the subject is a proposition which is self-evident *simpliciter* and since knowing the *quidditas* of a subject entails and is entailed by knowing all of its essential properties, it would appear that on Aquinas' view we can state the conditions for knowing the meaning or nature of the subject and predicate of a proposition which is self-evident *simpliciter* by saying something like the following:

(C) *x* knows the meaning or nature of the subject A and the predicate B of a proposition which is self-evident *simpliciter* if and only if for *every* proposition P which contains either A or B and which is self-evident *simpliciter*, *x* knows that P is self-evident *simpliciter*, i.e., *x* knows that the predicate of P is included in the meaning or nature of the subject of P.

Now since by (C) it is a necessary condition of knowing the meaning or nature of the subject of the proposition in (f) that we know *every* proposition about God which is self-evident *simpliciter,* it may very well be true that no one knows the meaning or nature of the subject of the proposition in (f) because it may very well be true that no one knows *every* proposition about God which is self-evident *simpliciter.* On the other hand, it may very well be true that we know or that some of us know the meaning or nature of the subjects and predicates of the propositions in (a) through (e) because it may very well be true that we know or that some of us know *every* proposition about those subjects and predicates which is self-evident *simpliciter.* However, it is not at all obvious how we could ever *determine* with respect to *any* subject that we know every proposition about that subject which is self-evident *simpliciter.* On the contrary, it seems obvious that we could never determine such a thing.

So, if (C) accurately states the conditions which Aquinas regards as being both necessary and sufficient for knowing the meaning or nature of the subject and predicate of a proposition which is self-evident *simpliciter,* then we could never determine whether or not we do know the meaning or nature of the subject and predicate of a proposition which is self-evident *simpliciter* and, hence, we could never determine whether or not a proposition is self-evident to us by 2.2. Accordingly, Aquinas' defense fails on the grounds that we could never determine that we do not know the meaning or nature of the subject of the proposition in (f) and, so, he has failed to show that the proposition 'God exists' is not self-evident to us.

But perhaps (C) is too strong a statement of the conditions which Aquinas regards as being both necessary and sufficient for knowing the meaning or nature of the subject and predicate of a proposition which is self-evident *simpliciter.* Perhaps, contrary to what would appear to be the case, we could say for Aquinas that knowing the *quidditas* of a subject does *not* entail knowing *all* of its essential properties. But, then, it is not obvious what conditions *are* necessary and sufficient for knowing the meaning or nature of the subject and predicate of a proposition which is self-evident *simpliciter* such that those conditions obtain for the subjects and predicates of the propositions in (a) through (e) but do not obtain for the subject of the proposition in (f). It may very well be, for example, that we do know and can determine that we know the *quidditas* of the subjects and predicates of the propositions in (a) through (e) though we do not know or cannot determine that we know *all* of their essential properties. Indeed, it seems reasonable to suggest that we do know the *quidditas* of the subjects and predicates of the propositions in (a) through (e) to the extent that we know that the propositions in (a) through (e) are self-evident *simpliciter*. So, perhaps we could say that we know the *quidditas* of the subject and predicate of a proposition which is self-evident *simpliciter* when we know that the proposition is self-evident *simpliciter*.

However, this principle does not distinguish the propositions in (a) through (e) from the proposition in (f) because Aquinas agrees that we know or can know that the proposition in (f) is self-evident *simpliciter*. So, it would follow from this principle and Aquinas' position on the proposition in (f) that we also know or can know the *quidditas* of God to the extent that we know that the proposition in (f) is self-evident *simpliciter* and that the proposition in (f) is self-evident to us just as are the propositions in (a) through (e). But Aquinas insists that we do not know the *quidditas* of God and that the proposition in (f) is *not* self-evident to us though the propositions in (a) through (e) are self-evident to us. Clearly, then, it will not do to say that we know the *quidditas* of the subject and predicate of a proposition which is self-evident *simpliciter* when we know that the proposition is self-evident *simpliciter*. What is not clear is what it is that we should say for Aquinas in order to specify the necessary and sufficient conditions for knowing the *quidditas* of the subject and predicate of a proposition which is self-evident *simpliciter* such that those conditions distinguish the propositions in (a) through (e) from the proposition in (f).

There is a fundamental difficulty with the suggestion that Aquinas is not committed to the principle that knowing the *quidditas* of a subject entails knowing *all* of its essential properties. The difficulty is that Aquinas provides no reason for thinking that there is any other kind of difference on his view between our knowledge or possible knowledge of the subjects and predicates of the propositions in (a) through (e) and our knowledge or possible knowledge of the subject of the proposition in (f). Aquinas provides no reason at all for thinking that there is any principle other than (C) which would justify rejecting the view that our knowledge of the terms in (a) through (f) is such that in whatever sense we know the meaning or nature of the terms in (a) through (e) we also know the meaning or nature of the subject term in (f), and in whatever sense we do *not* know the meaning or nature of the subject term in (f) we also do *not* know the meaning or nature of the terms in (a) through (e). So, if (C) is too strong a statement of the conditions which Aquinas regards as being both necessary and sufficient for knowing the meaning or nature of the subject and predicate of a proposition which is self-evident *simpliciter,* then, since Aquinas provides no other reason for supposing that knowing the *quidditas* of a subject entails a set of conditions which are not satisfied by the subject of the proposition in (f), it follows that he has not made out a case for saying that we do not know the *quidditas* of God. Accordingly, Aquinas has failed to show that the proposition 'God exists' is not self-evident to us by 2.2.

However, even if this difficulty could be overcome, Aquinas still would not have succeeded in establishing his thesis because it would appear that 2.2 entails a contradiction. In 2.2 Aquinas is making two claims. First, he is claiming that if the condition obtains that we know the meaning or nature of the subject and predicate of a proposition that is self-evident *simpliciter,* then the proposition is self-evident to us. That is to say, he is claiming that if the condition in question obtains, then we know that the proposition is true simply by virtue of the fact that the condition in question obtains. But, second, Aquinas is claiming that not only is it sufficient but that it is also *necessary* that the condition in question obtains in order for it to be the case that the proposition is self-evident to us. That is to say, Aquinas insists that

(N) a proposition is self-evident in such a way that we know that the proposition is true simply by virtue of the fact that it is self-evident in that way *only if* the condition obtains that we know the meaning or nature of the subject and predicate of the proposition.

For Aquinas no other condition is or can be sufficient. For even if Aquinas could establish that we do *not* know the meaning or nature of the subject of the proposition in (f), he would *not* have established that the proposition in (f) is not self-evident to us *unless* it is indeed true that being self-evident by the condition of 2.2 is the *only* way in which a proposition can be self-evident such that we know that the proposition is true simply by virtue of the fact that it is self-evident in that way. In other words, Aquinas' defense of his thesis *requires* that (N) be true.

But, now, it would appear that 2.2 entails that (N) is *not* true. For, by the first claim of 2.2 Aquinas maintains that a proposition is self-evident to us *if* the condition obtains that we know the meaning or nature of the subject and predicate of the proposition and the proposition is self-evident *simpliciter.* But the statement that we know the meaning or nature of the subject and predicate of a proposition whose predicate is included in the meaning or nature of the subject does not entail that we know that the proposition is true *unless* it is also true that

    (i) a proposition whose predicate is included in the meaning or nature of its subject is true simply by virtue of the fact that its predicate is included in the meaning or nature of its subject (i.e., a proposition that is self-evident *simpliciter* is true simply by virtue of the fact that it is self-evident *simpliciter*), and

    (ii) we know *that* a proposition whose predicate is included in the meaning or nature of its subject is true simply by virtue of the fact that its predicate is included in the meaning or nature of its subject (i.e., we know *that* a proposition that is self-evident *simpliciter* is true simply by virtue of the fact that it is self-evident *simpliciter*).

In other words, the first claim of 2.2 entails (i) and (ii).

But, then, from (i) and (ii) it would appear to follow that if a proposition satisfies the set of conditions C2, then the proposition is self-evident to us. That is, it would appear to follow that

    (M) a proposition is self-evident in such a way that we know that the proposition is true simply by virtue of the fact that it is self-evident in that way *if* the proposition is self-evident *simpliciter* and we know that the proposition is self-evident *simpliciter*.

This is so because it would appear to follow from (i) and (ii) that if we know *that* a proposition is self-evident *simpliciter,* then we know *of* that proposition that it is true simply by virtue of the fact that it is self-evident *simpliciter* and we know *this* simply by virtue of the fact that we know *that* the proposition is self-evident *simpliciter.* So, since the first claim of 2.2 entails (i) and (ii) and since (i) and (ii) jointly entail (M), it follows that the first claim of 2.2 entails (M). However, if (M) is true then (N) is *not* true. It turns out, then, that the first claim of 2.2 entails (M) and that the second claim of 2.2 asserts (N). But (M) and (N) cannot both be true. So, 2.2 entails a contradiction and, hence, 2.2 is false. Accordingly, even if Aquinas could show that we do not know the meaning or nature of the subject of the proposition in (f), he would not have succeeded in showing that the proposition in (f) is not self-evident to us in the required way; and he would not have succeeded because 2.2 is false.

Furthermore, it would not help Aquinas to modify his position by rejecting one of the claims of 2.2. For if Aquinas were to reject the first claim of 2.2, then 2.2 would simply state what condition is *necessary* in order for a proposition to be self-evident to us. But without knowing the *sufficient* conditions, we would never know whether or not *any* proposition is self-evident to us in the required way. On the other hand, if Aquinas were to reject the second claim of 2.2 in favor of the first claim, then, since the first claim of 2.2 entails (M) and (M) entails 2.1, the proposition in (f), 'God exists,' would turn out, on Aquinas' view, to be self-evident to us. This is so because Aquinas maintains that the proposition in (f) is self-evident *simpliciter* and that we know, or can know, that it is self-evident *simpliciter*.

The final result, then, is that Aquinas' explication of the difference between his two ways of being self-evident suffers from two fatal flaws and, hence, the explication fails to sustain his thesis about the self-evidence of God's existence. On the one hand, we could never determine whether or not a proposition is self-evident to us by appealing to 1.2 and 2.2 because we can never determine whether or not we ever do in fact know the meaning or nature of the subject and predicate of a proposition. So, we cannot determine whether or not the proposition in (f) is self-evident to us by appealing to 1.2 and 2.2. On the other hand, because 2.2 is false, we could never determine whether or not a proposition is self-evident to us by appealing to 1.2 and 2.2 even if we could determine whether or not we know the meaning or nature of the subject and predicate of the proposition. So, again, we cannot determine whether or not the proposition in (f) is self-evident to us by appealing to 1.2 and 2.2.

Now, since there is no apparent difference between our knowledge of the subjects and predicates of the propositions in (a) through (e) and our knowledge of the subject of the proposition in (f) and since no apparent modification of 2.2 will help Aquinas to sustain his position, it turns out that the explication which Aquinas gives of the difference between his two ways of being self-evident does not foreclose the possibility of holding that the existence of God is self-evident in such a way that God's existence needs no demonstration. Indeed, one could plausibly elect to hold the proposition 'God exists' is self-evident to us by appealing to 1.1 and 2.1. For if (i) and (ii) are true and Aquinas is correct in maintaining that the proposition 'God exists' is self-evident *simpliciter* and that we know that the proposition is self-evident *simpliciter*, then it would appear to follow that the proposition 'God exists' is self-evident in such a way that we know that the proposition is true simply by virtue of the fact that it is self-evident in that way and, hence, that the existence of God needs no demonstration. So, Aquinas has failed to show that the existence of God is not self-evident in any way that would hinder his program of rational theology because the possibility remains that the existence of God is self-evident in such a way that it needs no demonstration.

However, just how great a hindrance this possibility is to Aquinas' program is not at all clear. That Aquinas thought it important is obvious from his efforts to argue against it, but it is not at all clear that any of Aquinas' predecessors or contemporaries ever actually held the view that the existence of God is self-evident in such a way that it needs no demonstration. To be sure, Aquinas represents certain philosophers as propounding that view, but there are serious questions concerning the accuracy of Aquinas' representations of those philosophers. If there are no arguments which actually purport to show that the existence of God is self-evident in such a way that it needs no demonstration, then it would appear that there are no actual impediments to Aquinas' program. The possibility that there are such arguments certainly shows that it is possible that there are impediments to Aquinas' program, but how this possibility prevents Aquinas' enterprise certainly needs to be explained. So, whether the issue is a real one or only a possible one is not really clear, nor is it clear how great a hindrance the possibility is to Aquinas' program. But this question and its attendant problems must be reserved for another time.

8

Omniprescience and Divine Determinism

In this essay I will try to show that there are what would appear to be some unnoticed consequences of the doctrine of divine foreknowledge. For the purposes of this discussion I will simply assume that future events (while future) are possible objects of knowledge and, hence, that fore-knowledge is possible. Accordingly, I will not be concerned with discussing such questions as the status of truth-values for future contingent propositions or whether knowledge is justified true belief. Furthermore, I will not be concerned with the issues involved in the claim that the doctrine of divine foreknowledge conflicts with doctrines concerning the properties of created beings, e.g., the doctrine of voluntary human action.

What I will try to show is that the doctrine of divine foreknowledge is incompatible with a cluster of other doctrines concerning certain properties of God. I will argue that God cannot possess all the properties ascribed to him in the cluster of doctrines in question when the doctrine of divine foreknowledge is added to that cluster and when divine foreknowledge is considered in relationship to or as being qualified by the other properties ascribed to God in that cluster of doctrines as I shall interpret it. I will not argue that anyone is in fact committed to subscribing to the cluster of doctrines in question as I interpret it, but only that no one can subscribe to it consistently. If my reasoning is correct it will follow that consistent theism must reject one of the doctrines in the cluster, or bring the doc-

From *Religious Studies* 12 (1976): 365–81. Reprinted by permission of Cambridge University Press.

trines into harmony by a different interpretation or analysis, or reject the assumption about the possibility of knowing future events.

The cluster of doctrines which I want to consider consists of the doctrines that

(A) God has foreknowledge,

(B) God is omniscient,

(C) God is immutable,

(D) God is eternal, and

(E) God decides (chooses, intends, purposes, etc.) to perform the acts he does perform.

Now, although I do not have a complete analysis specifying both the necessary and sufficient conditions of what it is to have foreknowledge, to be omniscient, to be immutable, to be eternal, to decide (choose, intend, purpose, etc.), or to perform an act, it seems reasonable to suppose that there are certain minimal conditions which are necessary (if not sufficient) for these properties to be ascribed to a divine being. For example, while it would seem that being omnipotent would entail having the power or ability to perform certain acts though it would not entail actually performing those acts, having foreknowledge and being omniscient would seem to entail not only having the ability to know certain things but also actually knowing those things. So, by the assumption that future events (while future) are possible objects of knowledge, knowing at least one event that will occur in the future would seem to be a necessary condition for the truth of (A). In other words, even in the absence of a complete analysis of what it is to have foreknowledge, it seems unexceptionable to suppose that any time at which it would be true to ascribe to God *no* knowledge of *any* future events, would also be a time at which it would be false to say of him that he has foreknowledge. One consequence of the doctrine of divine foreknowledge would seem to be that there must be *at least one* future event among the objects of God's knowledge.

This consequence, however, is not one of the unnoticed ones and is hardly startling, for an even stronger consequence follows from the assumption about future events as objects of knowledge and the doctrine of divine omniscience. No matter how we are to characterize what constitutes an object of knowledge, it would appear reasonable to suppose that any condition under which it would be false to ascribe to God the knowledge of some event or other, would also be a condition under which it would be false to say of him that he is omniscient. To be omniscient God must have knowledge of *all* events. So, if it is false to ascribe to God the knowledge of some *future* event or other, then it would also be false to say of him that he is omniscient. The doctrine that God is omniscient, then, when taken together with the assumption about future events, entails that there must be at least one future event among the objects of God's knowledge because it entails that *all* future events must be among the objects of God's knowledge. Having foreknowledge entails having knowledge of *at least one* future event, but being omniscient *and* having foreknowledge entails having knowledge of *all* future events. In short (B) and the assumption about future events jointly entail that God's foreknowledge is to be understood as foreknowledge of *all* future events and I will refer to this as the doctrine that

(A′) God is omniprescient.

So far, then, on the assumption that future events are in principle knowable, the modest consequence of the doctrine of divine foreknowledge would appear to be that divine foreknowledge is an aspect or function of divine omniscience and is, accordingly, to be understood as divine omniprescience. But as we have interpreted it up to this point, the doctrine of divine omniprescience is compatible with the claim that God is *now* omniprescient while he *was not* omniprescient, say, prior to creation and *will not* be omniprescient, say, at the day of judgment. All that is required for God to be omniprescient *now* is that he *now* have knowledge of all future events and this is compatible with his having acquired the knowledge of all future events yesterday and his losing the knowledge of some future events tomorrow. So, it is possible that while (A′) is true *now* it was not true at some time in the past and will not be true at some time in the future. On the present understanding of divine omniprescience it is possible that omniprescience is a property which God has at one time but does not have at another time. But to possess a property at one time and not at another time is to be subject to change and according to doctrine (C) God is immutable.

Now, it is difficult to find an adequate analysis of divine immutability because such an analysis must admit as allowable certain *kinds* of change in God but not others, and it must provide a *general* criterion for distinguishing just those properties with respect to which change of *some* kind is to be allowed in God from just those properties with respect to which *no* kind of change is to be allowed in God. Nevertheless, even in the absence of such an analysis it seems reasonable to suppose that the doctrine of divine immutability applies with respect to the properties ascribed to God in (A') and (B) though, perhaps, it does not apply with respect to certain other properties of God. On an intuitive understanding of divine immutability it seems reasonable to allow that *it is not the case* that just *any* situation in which it would be true to ascribe to God the possession of a property at one time but not at another time, would also be a situation in which it would be false to say of him that he is immutable. Perhaps, as a matter of fact, there are properties God could possess at one time but not at another time and still be counted as immutable. For example, perhaps the situation in which God possesses at one time but not at another time the property of being loved by St. Paul would be a situation which we could count as being consistent with the claim that God is immutable.[1] After all, possessing at one time but not at another time the property of being loved by St. Paul would not seem to alter God substantially. But it also seems reasonable to allow that under exactly the same understanding of divine immutability *any* situation in which it would be true to ascribe to God the possession of omniprescience at one time but not at another time, *would* be a situation in which it would be false to say of him that he is immutable. After all, possessing at one time but not at another time the property of being omniprescient *would* seem to alter God substantially. It seems reasonable to suppose that if God is immutable, then omniprescience is *not* a property he can possess at one time and not at another time. On the assumption that God is immutable and on an intuitive understanding of divine immutability and divine omniprescience, it would appear to follow that if God is *ever* omniprescient, then he is *always* omniprescient. So, when taken together with the doctrine of divine immutability, the doctrine of divine omniprescience is to be understood as the doctrine that God has knowledge of *all* future events at *every* moment of his duration, that there is *no time* in his history at which God does *not* have knowledge of *all* future events.

Furthermore, this understanding of the doctrine of divine omniprescience can be made even more precise if we also consider divine omniprescience in relationship to the doctrine of divine eternity. On our present understanding, the doctrine of divine omniprescience is consistent with there being a time at which it was false that God had knowledge of all future events. If God exists and is both immutable and omniprescient, then it is false that he can ever fail to have knowledge of all future events.

However, if God began to exist at some time, then, while it is true that he cannot fail to be omniprescient throughout his existence, there was a time prior to his existence at which it was false that God had knowledge of all future events. Now while the doctrine of divine eternity is subject to at least two interpretations, it is clear that however it is to be interpreted the doctrine that God is eternal excludes the possibility of significant reference to time prior to God's existence and a consideration of that doctrine will have some bearing on our understanding of God's attributes in general and divine omniprescience in particular. On the first interpretation, the eternity of God is explained as unending duration. According to this view the existence of God extends indefinitely both forward and backward *in time* and temporal predications are both logically and linguistically appropriate in ascribing attributes to God. On the second interpretation, the eternity of God is explained as "timelessness." According to this view the existence of God has "no duration" because God is "*outside of time*" and temporal predications are either logically or linguistically *in*appropriate in ascribing attributes to God. On the first interpretation, propositions are false which refer to time prior to God's existence because time is indefinitely extended in both directions and God exists at every moment in time. On the second interpretation, it is inappropriate to refer to time prior to God's existence because God exists outside of time and is not related to anything by time. On both of these interpretations, then, it is a mistake to refer to time prior to God's existence and, hence, it is also a mistake to claim that there was a time prior to God's existence at which it was false that God had knowledge of all future events. So, when taken together with the doctrine of divine eternity, the doctrine of divine omniprescience must be stated in such a way as to reflect the fact that divine omniprescience is a property of an eternal being that never fails to exist.

If we adopt the first interpretation of divine eternity, then temporal predications are appropriate in stating the doctrine of divine omniprescience. On the other hand, if we adopt the second interpretation of divine eternity, then temporal predications are inappropriate in stating the doctrine of divine omniprescience. For the purposes of the present discussion I propose to adopt the first interpretation. I do this for two reasons. First, while both interpretations are reasonable enough, I think that the first is more widely held, and perhaps more coherently explainable, than the other interpretation. Second, I am confident that most of the consequences I will point out follow under either interpretation.[2] My subsequent arguments rest on the assumption that certain acts are in time and occur at particular times and, hence, that the consequences follow because an omniprescient being with unending duration could not perform those acts. So, if the omniprescient being is outside of time and if my assumptions are correct about the temporal aspects of certain acts, then the same consequences will follow because an omniprescient being outside of time could not perform those acts that are in time and occur at particular times.[3] Adopting the first interpretation of the doctrine of divine eternity, then, God has unending duration and the doctrine of divine omniprescience is to be understood as the doctrine that God has knowledge of *all* future events at *every* moment of an indefinite stretch of time, that there is *no time at all, ever,* at which God does *not* have knowledge of *all* future events.

Now while there are undoubtedly a number of both direct and indirect consequences which follow from this understanding of the doctrine of divine omniprescience, there are two direct consequences and their results to which I want to devote particular attention. It seems quite clear that this understanding of the doctrine of divine omniprescience entails both that

(P1) For *any* act that God performs there is *no* time prior to that act at which God does *not* know that he will perform that act; and

(P2) If God knows at T_1 that he will do (will not do) a at T_3, then at T_2 or T_3 it is not possible for God to refrain from doing (to do) a at T_3.

The doctrine of divine omniprescience entails (P1) because if (P1) is false then at some time God performs an act that he did not, at some time prior to the act, know he was going to perform and, hence, it is false that God *always* knows *all* future events. But by the doctrine of divine omniprescience God *always* knows *all* future events. So, if (P1) is false, then God is *not* omniprescient and the doctrine of divine omniprescience and the falsity of (P1) jointly entail that God is both omniprescient *and* not omniprescient. The doctrine of divine omniprescience entails (P2) because if (P2) is false then it is possible for God to do each one of two things, namely, *know* at T_1 that he will do a at T_3 and also refrain from doing a at T_3. But by the doctrine of divine omniprescience, if God refrains from doing a at T_3, then God knows at T_1 that he will refrain from doing a at T_3. So, if (P2) is false, then it is possible for God to do each one of two things, namely, know at T_1 that he *will* do a at T_3 and also know at T_1 that he *will not* do a at T_3. Furthermore, by the doctrine of divine omniprescience, if God *knows* at T_1 that he *will* do *a* at T_3, then God *does* do *a* at T_3 (otherwise he cannot know at T_1 that he will). So, if (P2) is false, then it is possible for God to do each one of two things, namely, *do a* at T_3 and also *refrain* from doing *a* at T_3. Since the truth of (A′) and the falsity of (P1) jointly entail a contradiction and since the truth of (A′) and the falsity of (P2) jointly entail a contradiction, it follows that both (P1) and (P2) are direct consequences of the doctrine of divine omniprescience. In addition to this, it would also appear to be the case that the doctrine that God is omniprescient is inconsistent with the doctrine that God decides (chooses, intends, purposes, etc.) to perform the acts he does perform. It would appear to be an indirect consequence of the doctrine of divine omniprescience that God *cannot* decide to perform the acts he does perform when (P1) and (P2) are taken together with certain assumptions about what it is to make a decision.

There are probably numerous factors to be accounted for in specifying both the necessary *and* sufficient conditions that obtain when what is usually regarded as a decision or free choice occurs. While it is most difficult to be certain that all those factors are enumerated in any given attempt at a complete analysis of what it is to make a decision, it seems reasonable to suppose that there are at least three factors present in a typical case of what is ordinarily regarded as decision making. First, decisions are typically *in* time and occur at *particular* times.[4] At least part of the significance of this temporal feature of what it is to make a decision is that when an individual makes a decision he decides at one time to either perform or refrain from performing a particular act at another time and there is a time prior to the decision in question when the individual has not yet decided what he is going to do with respect to the act in question. In other words, in decision making there is typically a period of time in which the issue in the decision either has not yet been considered or is being deliberated and, hence, has not yet been decided, and this period is *prior* to the decision. So, it would seem that one typical characteristic of decision making can be expressed in quite general terms by saying that

(Q1) '*x* decides at T_2 to do *a* at T_3' entails 'there is a time, T_1, prior to T_2, at which *x* has not yet decided with respect to doing *a* at T_3.'

Second, decisions typically involve our acts in the future about which we are uncertain. At least part of the significance of this feature of what it is to make a decision is that when an individual makes a decision he decides at one time to either perform or refrain from performing a particular act at another time, and prior to the decision, when he has not yet decided with respect to performing the act, he does not know whether or not he will perform the act. In other words, an individual cannot both be undecided with respect to performing some future act and at the same time know that he will perform that act. For, while the fact that an individual *now* knows that he will perform some act a at some time in the future does *not* entail that he has decided to do a at that time, it seems reasonable to suppose that if an individual does *now* know that he will do a at some time in the future then either no decision is even possible with respect to doing a (and, hence, it cannot be said either that he is decided or that he is undecided) or he cannot be undecided with respect to doing a at that time. Because if an individual *now* knows that he will do a at some time in the future, then he knows it either because he knows that he is constrained in some way to do a or because he has already decided to do a at that time. But if an individual *now* knows that he will do a at some time in the future because he knows that he is constrained in some way to do a at that time, then, while he may be perfectly willing to do a whether or not constrained, no decision is even possible for him with respect to doing a at that time (so, he can neither be said to be decided nor be said to be undecided with respect to doing a). On the other hand, if an individual *now* knows that he will do a at some time in the future because he has already decided to do a at that time, then while he can change his mind or reconsider, he cannot both stand on his decision maintaining his knowledge that he will do a and at the same time be undecided with respect to doing a at that time. It seems clear, then, that an individual cannot both be undecided at T_1 with respect to doing a at T_3 and know at T_1 that he will do a at T_3. If an individual has not yet decided at T_1 with respect to doing a at T_3, then he does not know at T_1 that he will do a at T_3. So, it would seem that another typical characteristic of decision making can be expressed in quite general terms by saying that

(Q2) 'x has not yet decided at T_1 with respect to doing a at T_3' entails 'x does not know at T_1 whether or not he will do a at T_3.'

Third, decisions typically involve either acts with respect to which there are genuine alternatives for acting or else acts with respect to which it is believed that there are genuine alternatives for action. At least part of the significance of this feature of what it is to make a decision is that when an individual makes a decision he decides at one time to either perform or refrain from performing a particular act at another time and he either knows or at least believes at the time of decision that it is both possible for him to perform the act *and* possible for him to refrain from performing the act. In other words, when an individual decides with respect to performing some future act he selects one of which he either knows or believes to be two real choices for acting. If an individual knows or believes at T_2 that he *cannot* perform a at T_3 or he knows or believes at T_2 that he *cannot refrain* from performing a at T_3 then he knows or believes at T_2 that there are no real choices with respect to doing a at T_3 and, hence, no decision is even possible at T_2 with respect to doing a at T_3. Conversely, if it is possible for an individual to decide at T_2 with respect to doing a at T_3, then either there are genuine alternatives at T_2 with respect to doing a at T_3 or there are no alternatives at T_2 with respect to doing a at T_3 and the individual does *not* know that there are no such alternatives. So it would seem that a further typical characteristic of decision making can be expressed in quite general terms by saying that

(Q3) 'It is possible for x to decide at T_2 to do a at T_3' entails 'either (i) it is possible at T_2 for x to do a at T_3 and it is possible at T_2 for x to refrain from doing a at T_3, or (ii) it is not possible at T_2 for x to do a at T_3 and x does not know it, or it is not possible at T_2 for x to refrain from doing a at T_3 and x does not know it.'

Though the preceding observations about decision making cannot be regarded as constituting a complete analysis of what it is to make a decision, it does not seem at all unwarranted to say that (Q1), (Q2), and (Q3) state at least some of the necessary conditions that must obtain in any case that is to be regarded as a case of decision making. If there is any situation in which one of these conditions fails to hold, then it would appear that no decision is possible in that situation. So, if my observations are correct concerning what it is to make a decision, then it would appear that an omniprescient being cannot make decisions because it is false that all these conditions can at some time obtain for an omniprescient being. When the direct consequences (P1) and (P2) of the doctrine of divine omniprescience are taken together with the necessary conditions (Q1), (Q2), and (Q3) of making a decision, it turns out to be an indirect consequence of the doctrine of divine omniprescience that God's acts cannot be the result of his choosing or deciding to perform those acts because it is not possible for God to decide or choose at all. There are two arguments for this conclusion.

The first argument requires (P1), (Q1), and (Q2) and can be represented schematically as follows:

I   (1) If it is possible for God to decide at T_2 to do a at T_3, then God has not yet decided at T_1 with respect to doing a at T_3 [by (Q1)].

      (2) If God has not yet decided at T_1 with respect to doing a at T_3, then God does not know at T_1 whether or not he will do a at T_3 [by (Q2)].

      (3) If it is possible for God to decide at T_2 to do a at T_3, then God does not know at T_1 whether or not he will do a at T_3 [from (1) and (2)].

      (4) It is false that God does not know at T_1 whether or not he will do a at T_3 [by (P1)].

      (5) It is not possible for God to decide at T_2 to do a at T_3 [from (3) and (4)].

The second argument for this conclusion requires (P1), (P2), (Q3), and (B) and can be represented schematically as follows:

II   (1) If it is possible for God to decide at T_2 to do a at T_3, then either (i) it is possible at T_2 for God to do a at T_3 *and* it is possible at T_2 for God to refrain from doing a at T_3, or (ii) one of these possibilities fails to obtain *and* God does not know that it fails to obtain [by (Q3)].

      (2) It is false that one of these possibilities fails to obtain *and* God does not know that it fails to obtain, i.e., (ii) of premise (1) is false [by (B)].

      (3) If it is possible for God to decide at T_2 to do a at T_3, then it is possible at T_2 for God to do a at T_3 *and* it is possible at T_2 for God to refrain from doing a at T_3 [from (1) and (2)].

      (4) If God does a at T_3, then God knows at T_1 that he will do a at T_3 [by (P1)].

      (5) If God knows at T_1 that he will do a at T_3, then it is not possible at T_2 for God to refrain from doing a at T_3 [by (P2)].

      (6) If God does *not* do a at T_3, then God knows at T_1 that he will *not* do a at T_3 [by (P1)].

      (7) If God knows at T_1 that he will not do a at T_3, then it is *not* possible at T_2 for God to do a at T_3 [by (P2)].

(8) If God does *a* at T_3, then it is *not* possible at T_2 for God to refrain from doing *a* at T_3 [from (4) and (5)].
(9) If God does *not* do *a* at T_3, then it is *not* possible at T_2 for God to do *a* at T_3 [from (6) and (7)].
(10) Either God does *a* at T_3 or God does *not* do *a* at T_3.
(11) Either it is *not* possible at T_2 for God to do *a* at T_3 or it is *not* possible at T_2 for God to refrain from doing *a* at T_3 [from (8), (9), and (10)].
(12) It is not possible for God to decide at T_2 to do *a* at T_3 [from (3) and (11)].

Since these two arguments and their identical conclusions apply indifferently both to every moment of the indefinite duration of God's existence and to every act that God performs, it is a consequence of the doctrine of divine omniprescience that it is impossible for God ever to make any decisions at all and that none of God's acts can be the result of his deciding or choosing to perform those acts. It turns out that when foreknowledge is considered as a property belonging to a being who is also omniscient, immutable, and eternal, then divine foreknowledge is to be understood as divine omniprescience and the doctrine of divine omniprescience is inconsistent with the doctrine that God decides (chooses, intends, purposes, etc.) to perform the acts he does perform. In short, the original cluster of doctrines concerning God's properties is inconsistent when divine foreknowledge is understood as being qualified by the present interpretation of divine omniscience, divine immutability, and divine eternity.

Furthermore, since by (P1) God knows from eternity every act that he will ever perform and every act that he will never perform it follows from (P2) that it is impossible for God ever to refrain from performing any act that he does perform and impossible for God ever to perform any act that he does not perform.[5] So, it is a consequence of the doctrine of divine omniprescience that God could neither decide to refrain or actually refrain from performing any of the acts he does perform nor decide to perform or actually perform any of the acts he does *not* perform. It would appear to follow, then, as a consequence of the doctrine of divine omniprescience, that *there is no divine free will.* Now, while this consequence, divine determinism, is almost surely to be regarded as unacceptable by most traditional theists, it is strangely compatible with the further widely received doctrine that God is a necessary being. According to the doctrine of divine necessity, God exists necessarily and possesses his properties in some necessary manner. By the present understanding of the doctrine of divine omniprescience it would also be the case that God performs the acts that he does perform by necessity. So, the doctrine of divine omniprescience and its consequent divine determinism is compatible with and even complements the doctrine that God is a necessary being. Despite the compatibility of these two doctrines, though, few traditional theists would be prepared to accept the doctrine of divine omniprescience and its consequent divine determinism and every effort possible would be made to avoid the doctrine under its present interpretation. But there are other consequences of the doctrine of divine omniprescience and its implied divine fatalism and I want to discuss some of them briefly before considering whether or not there are any promising ways of avoiding the present understanding of the doctrine of divine omniprescience and its consequences.

First, it would appear to be a consequence of the doctrine of divine omniprescience that either God is *not* omnipotent or God is omnipotent and all humans are omnipotent as well. In order to make this consequence clear, let us consider the assumption that it is a necessary condition for an agent to be omnipotent that he have it within his power *either* to refrain from performing *at least one* of the acts that he actually does perform *or* to perform *at least one* of the acts that he actually does not perform. If we accept the assumption, then it follows that God is not omnipotent. For, as we have already observed, if God is omniprescient then it is not within his power to make decisions and it is not even within his power either to perform *any* of the acts he does not perform or to refrain from performing *any* of the acts he does perform. So, if we accept the assumption, then it follows that if God is omniprescient then he is *not* omnipotent. On the other hand, if we reject the assumption, then divine omnipotence is consistent with the divine determinism implied by the doctrine of divine omniprescience. But by divine determinism what God has the power or ability to do is simply perform those acts that he does in fact perform. So, since the doctrine that God is omnipotent is a doctrine about God's power and ability, the doctrine of divine omnipotence reduces to the doctrine that God's power consists in being able to perform any act that he in fact performs. Now whether or not human determinism follows from the doctrine of divine omniprescience, it is true at the very least to say that any human's power consists in being able to perform any act that he in fact performs. But, then, it would appear to follow that all humans are omnipotent. So, if we reject the assumption, then it follows that if God is omniprescient then he is omnipotent and all humans are omnipotent as well. Since we must either accept the assumption or reject it, a further consequence of the doctrine of divine omniprescience is that either God is *not* omnipotent or God is omnipotent and all humans are omnipotent as well.[6]

Second, some of the consequences of the doctrine of divine omniprescience that have already been mentioned also have a bearing on how we are to understand the doctrine that God is omnibenevolent. The doctrine of divine omnibenevolence is intended to entail at the very least both that God is intrinsically good and that *all* of God's acts are good either because they are intrinsically good or because they are intended to bring about a greater intrinsic good. Now while it is not entirely clear how we are to understand the claim that God is intrinsically good or the claim that *all* of God's acts are good, it should be clear that under the doctrine of divine omniprescience God's intrinsic goodness cannot be explained in terms of the goodness of God's acts. It will not do to say that God's intrinsic goodness consists wholly or even partly in the fact that God performs *all* of the acts that he does perform on the grounds that they are good. To perform an act on the grounds that it has some special feature is to perform that act as a result of *deciding,* because of that special feature, to perform that particular act and not some other act instead. In other words, performing an act on the grounds that it has some special feature entails performing that act as a result of deciding to perform that act and this in turn entails that it is within the power of the agent to decide. So performing an act on the grounds that it is good, entails having it within one's power to decide, at least with respect to the act in question. But, since it is not within God's power to make any decisions at all, it follows that God cannot perform *any* acts on the grounds that there are reasons or motives for performing those acts. So, God cannot perform *any* acts on the grounds that they are good. Even if all of God's acts are in fact good, it cannot be because of the goodness of those acts that God performs them and, hence, God's intrinsic goodness cannot consist, even in part, in the fact that God performs all of the acts that he does perform on the grounds that they are good.

Furthermore, it will not do to say that God's intrinsic goodness consists simply in the fact that all of his acts are good. To say that God is good *because* all of his acts are good entails that God's goodness is a function of the quality of his acts and derives from the quality of his acts. But then if God's goodness is a function of and derives from the quality of his acts, then God's goodness is contingent and not intrinsic and this attempted explanation is not an explanation of God's *intrinsic* goodness at all. If God's moral quality is a function of the quality of his acts, then God would become malevolent or less than intrinsically good if he were to perform malevolent acts.

Moreover, this attempt to explain God's intrinsic goodness cannot be salvaged by adding that while God's moral quality is a function of the quality of his acts, God's goodness is nevertheless intrinsic and not contingent because all of God's acts are necessary and, hence, are necessarily good. Even if all of God's acts up to the present time are in fact good and even though by divine determinism all of God's acts are necessary, it does not follow that God's acts are necessarily good and that, hence, his goodness is intrinsic and not contingent. It is perfectly consistent with both divine determinism and the goodness of all of God's completed acts that at some time in the future he will perform some malevolent acts. The necessity of God's acts consists in his inability to refrain from performing the acts which he actually does perform and *not* in the quality of the acts which he is unable to refrain from performing. By divine determinism there is *nothing* that can prevent God from performing the acts that he does perform, but there is also *nothing* that can prevent him from performing malevolent acts. By divine determinism, then, God's acts are *not* necessarily good. So, it is possible for God to perform malevolent acts and if God's moral quality is a function of the quality of his acts, then God's goodness is contingent and not intrinsic, because it is possible for him to become malevolent. Even if all of God's acts are in fact good, it cannot be because of the goodness of all God's acts that he is intrinsically good and, hence, God's intrinsic goodness cannot consist in the fact that all of his acts are good. It would appear to follow, then, that under the doctrine that God is omniprescient, God's intrinsic goodness cannot be explained in terms of the goodness of his acts.

Indeed, it would appear to follow from the doctrine of divine omniprescience that there is no explanation at all of the claim that God is intrinsically good. By divine determinism it is impossible that God has performed any act which he might have refrained from performing.[7] It follows from this that if omniprescience is a property of God, then God cannot ever possess any *other* property which entails that it is possible that he has performed an act which he might have refrained from performing if he did not possess that property. So, if goodness is a property which entails that it is possible that an agent bearing the property has performed an act which he might have refrained from performing if he did not possess the property, then it is impossible for God ever to possess the property of being good. Similarly, if malevolence is a property which entails that it is possible that an agent bearing the property has performed an act which he might have refrained from performing if he did not possess the property, then it is impossible for God ever to possess the property of being malevolent. On the other hand, if goodness and malevolence are *not* properties which entail that it is possible that an agent bearing the property has performed an act which he might have refrained from performing if he did not possess the property, then divine goodness and divine malevolence are both consistent with any divine acts whatsoever whether the acts are good or whether the acts are evil. But if the distinction between divine goodness and divine malevolence entails no possible difference between which acts God will perform and which acts he will not perform, then there would appear to be no *genuine* distinction between divine omnibenevolence and divine malevolence.

So, if God is omniprescient, then it would appear to follow either that it is impossible for God to be good and it is impossible for God to be malevolent, or that there is no genuine distinction between divine omnibenevolence and divine malevolence. In either case it would seem reasonable to conclude that normative uses of the terms 'good' and 'evil' are as inappropriate when applied to God as they are when applied to gravity, and, hence, that there is no explanation of the claim that God is intrinsically good because the claim is inappropriate for an omniprescient being. So, it would appear to follow from the doctrine of divine omniprescience that God cannot perform any of his acts on the grounds that they are good, that it is possible for God to perform malevolent acts,[8] and that 'omnibenevolent' is a logically inappropriate predicate for God.

Third, the divine determinism implied by the doctrine of divine omniprescience also has a bearing on how we are to understand the doctrine that God is a person. Since God cannot perform *any* acts on the grounds that there are reasons or motives for performing those acts, it follows not only that God cannot perform any acts on the grounds that those acts are good, but also that God cannot perform any acts on the grounds that he, himself, has any particular property. So, for example, God cannot perform any acts on the grounds that he has the property of loving everyone or the property of hating everyone, or on the grounds that he has the property of being interested in the welfare of others or the property of being unconcerned about the welfare of others, or on the grounds that he has the property of being the one who punishes the wicked or the property of being the one who rewards the wicked. In short, God cannot perform any acts on the grounds that he has some property or its contrary which is a constituent of being a person.

Indeed, every property and its contrary which is a constituent of being a person either is a property which entails that it is possible that an agent bearing the property has performed an act he might have refrained from performing if he did not possess the property, or is a property that does not entail this. So, given any such property and its contrary for which the entailment holds, it follows that it is impossible for God ever to possess that given property and it is impossible for God ever to possess the contrary of that given property. Further, given any such property and its contrary for which the entailment does *not* hold, it follows that there is no genuine distinction between God's possessing that given property and his possessing the contrary of that given property. In either case it seems reasonable to conclude that terms designating properties and their contraries which are constituents of being a person ('hates,' 'loves,' and 'is indifferent,' for example) are as inappropriate when applied to God as they are when applied to gravity and, hence, that there is no explanation of the claim that God is a person because the claim is inappropriate for an omniprescient being. So, it would appear to be a consequence of the doctrine of divine omniprescience that God cannot perform any acts on the grounds that he has properties which are constituents of being a person and that 'person' is a logically inappropriate predicate for God.

Fourth, it is a consequence of the doctrine of divine omniprescience that there is no problem of evil. By divine determinism it is not within God's power to refrain from performing any of the acts that he does perform and it is not within God's power to perform any of the acts he does not perform. So, since God created this world and he created it with evil in it, it was not within God's power to refrain from creating this world and it was not within God's power to create it without evil.[9] In short, the existence of God is compatible with the existence of evil in the world, no matter how much evil there is, because God could not have acted differently when he created. So, it would appear to be the case that if God is omniprescient, then there is no problem of evil.

Now while these four consequences deserve a more detailed account than the limitations of a short paper have permitted, enough has been said, I think, to show that they follow from the divine determinism implied by the doctrine of divine omniprescience. Furthermore, these four consequences are not the only consequences of the doctrine of divine omniprescience. There are numerous other doctrines of traditional theism which are either inconsistent with or drastically modified by divine determinism. Under divine omniprescience such doctrines as, for example, the efficacy of prayer and human redemption are almost surely false, while such doctrines as, for example, the future beatitude of the soul and cosmological teleology are almost surely in need of severe reinterpretation. Though it is not possible to discuss or even mention all of these consequences here, it would appear to be the case that all of the consequences of the doctrine of divine omniprescience are either inconsistent with other doctrines of traditional theism or rest on consequences which are inconsistent with other doctrines of traditional theism. So, consistent theism must either reject all of the traditional doctrines which are incompatible with the doctrine of divine omniprescience or avoid the doctrine of divine omniprescience and its consequent divine determinism. Clearly, the latter way of achieving consistency would be more acceptable to traditional theism if there is any way at all to accomplish it.

But since divine omniprescience is entailed by the original cluster of doctrines when that cluster is taken together with the assumption that all future events are in principle knowable, it is possible to escape the doctrine that God is omniprescient only by either reinterpreting the original cluster of doctrines or rejecting the assumption that all future events are in principle knowable.[10] The first approach would not appear to be very promising though. For with the possible exception of the doctrine that God is eternal, the interpretation that has been placed on the original cluster of doctrines seems to be unexceptionable. If God is omniscient then he must surely know everything knowable, and if he is immutable then he must surely be changeless with respect to both his omniscience and his foreknowledge. The consequences of reinterpreting either one of these two doctrines would be as unacceptable to traditional theism as the consequences of divine omniprescience. Furthermore, since the doctrine of divine timelessness is fraught with as many difficulties for traditional theism as the doctrine of divine omniprescience, interpreting God's eternity as other than endless duration would not appear to provide a very promising way of escaping the claim that God is omniprescient. So, it would seem that the most promising approach in avoiding the doctrine of divine omniprescience and its divine determinism is to reject the claim that all future events are in principle knowable.

Indeed, there are two quite familiar ways of rejecting this assumption about the possibility of knowing *all* future events. There is a strong counterthesis which maintains that *no* future contingent events are knowable and there is a weaker counterthesis which maintains that *some* future contingent events are *not* knowable. The strong counterthesis is that future contingent propositions are neither true nor false. So, given that having knowledge entails the truth of the proposition expressing the knowledge claim, it follows that no future contingent proposition can express a knowledge claim and, hence, that knowledge about future contingent events is impossible. It would follow directly that since foreknowledge is in principle impossible, God cannot have foreknowledge because he cannot do the impossible. If this counterthesis can be sustained, then it provides a promising way of avoiding the doctrine of divine omniprescience and its divine determinism.

The weaker counterthesis is that if knowledge of future events is possible, then it must be inductive knowledge since, by hypothesis, it cannot be knowledge by direct acquaintance. But, then, it is possible to know only those future events which are subject to the laws of nature and predictability. So, if certain kinds of future events are not subject to the laws of nature and predictability, it follows that certain kinds of future events are in principle unknowable. Now, the reasoning continues, acts of sentient wills are events not subject to the laws of nature and predictability, so future acts of the will and any other acts caused by them are future events which are in principle unknowable. It follows from this that *no* sentient being can know what acts he or any other sentient being will perform in the future when those future acts are either acts of the will or caused by an act of the will.[11] So, while foreknowledge of some future events is possible, it would follow from this counterthesis that omniprescience is in principle impossible and that God cannot be omniprescient because he cannot do the impossible. If this counterthesis can be sustained, then it, too, provides a promising way of avoiding the doctrine of divine omniprescience and its divine determinism.

Without arguing the merits or demerits of these two counttheses I will simply point out that there is little agreement about them among philosophers. The problem of future contingent propositions is hardly settled and is still being debated. The same is true, of course, for the problem of the justification of knowledge. In fact, some philosophers, Nelson Pike[12] for example, urge that there are clear cases in which the verb 'knows' applies even though the knower does not have evidence or grounds for his belief, and, hence, that 'crystal-ball' knowledge of future events is not impossible. In any case, since it is not *a priori* true that all future events are in principle knowable, traditional theism does *not* entail the doctrine of divine omniprescience and its consequent divine determinism. Traditional theism can avoid divine determinism by adopting one of the countertheses about the possibility of knowing the future. However, if *all* future events *are* in principle knowable and God is omniscient, eternal, and immutable, then God is also omniprescient and completely determined.

NOTES

1. For an interesting discussion of God's immutability see Alvin Plantinga, *God and Other Minds* (Ithaca, N.Y.: Cornell University Press, 1967), pp. 173–80; and a critique of Plantinga in James Tomberlin, "Plantinga's Puzzles About God and Other Minds," *The Philosophical Forum* 1, no. 3 (Spring 1969, new series): 376–84. Subsequently Tomberlin amends part of Plantinga's argument to free it of some criticisms in "Omniscience and Necessity: Putting Humpty-Dumpty Together Again," *The Philosophical Forum* 2, no. 1 (Fall 1970, new series): 149–51 and I argue that Tomberlin's amendment fails in my article "God Might Not Love Us," *International Journal for Philosophy of Religion* 5, no. 3 (Fall 1974): 157–61.

2. Even if my confidence on this point turned out to be unjustified, the doctrine of God's eternity as timelessness, itself, has consequences as unacceptable to traditional theism as the consequences of the doctrine of divine omniprescience. For a comprehensive study of the doctrine of God as a timeless being see Nelson Pike, *God and Timelessness* (New York: Schocken Books Inc., 1970), hereafter cited as "Pike."

3. For a brief discussion of God's inability to perform certain temporal acts if he is timeless see Robert Coburn, "Professor Malcolm on God," *Australasian Journal of Philosophy* 41 (August 1963): 143–62, hereafter cited as "Coburn." See also a discussion of Coburn in Pike, pp. 121–29. These discussions develop points about timelessness and God's inability to perform certain acts which are similar to some of the points I will develop about unending duration and God's inability to perform certain acts.

4. If God is timeless it would seem to follow immediately that God cannot decide, choose, etc. See Coburn, p. 155.

5. If God is timeless and everything is "all at once timelessly present" to him, then all of his acts are timelessly present and there is no "time" at which he could have acted differently. So, a similar consequence would appear to follow if divine eternity is understood as timelessness.

6. For a further consideration of the claim that God cannot be both omniscient and omnipotent see my article "The Incompatibility of Omnipotence and Omniscience" in *Analysis* 33, no. 5 (April 1973), and my article "Omnipotence, Omniscience, and Necessity" in *Analysis* 34, no. 2 (December 1973).

7. It is interesting to notice that divine determinism does *not* entail that it is impossible that God has performed an act which he might *not* have performed. But while any given act of God is an act he might not have performed (he *might* have been determined to act differently) that act is *not* an act he could have *refrained* from performing.

8. Perhaps what we should say here is that the term 'act' and, hence, the terms 'good acts,' 'malevolent acts,' etc., are as inappropriate when describing the effects of God as they are when describing the effects of gravity.

9. For an argument that God's goodness is logically incompatible with evil in the world if God could have refrained from creating altogether, see my forthcoming article "Unjustified Evil, and God's Choice" in *Sophia* (Australia) 13 (April 1974).

10. I will not deal with the possibility of rejecting one of the doctrines in the cluster because that alternative would seem to be just as unacceptable for traditional theism as adopting the doctrine of divine omniprescience.

11. For a discussion which represents this type of view see Richard Taylor, "Deliberation and Foreknowledge," *American Philosophical Quarterly* 1, no. 1 (January 1964): 73–80.

12. See Pike, pp. 54–55.

9

The Impossibility of Defining 'Omnipotence'

It seems reasonable to insist that certain conditions must be satisfied by any definition of omnipotence if it is to be regarded as an adequate definition. First, it seems reasonable not to require of an omnipotent being that he be able to bring about a state of affairs that it is logically impossible to bring about. So, for example, we cannot reasonably require of an omnipotent being that he be able to bring about a state of affairs in which there exists a round square. Since the description of that state of affairs is self-contradictory, it is logically impossible that there should exist a state of affairs to which the description truly applies and, hence, it is logically impossible that there should be any action which can truly be described as bringing about that state of affairs. Accordingly, the claim that a being cannot bring about a state of affairs in which there exists a round square does not entail that the being lacks some power or ability and, hence, does not entail that the being is not omnipotent. It seems reasonable, then, to adopt the principle that the failure to bring about a state of affairs that it is logically impossible to bring about does not count against omnipotence or falsify the claim that a being is omnipotent. Some few philosophers like Descartes[1] and Wade Savage[2] are not ready to countenance the reasonableness of this principle, but Harry G. Frankfurt[3] has shown what logical absurdities follow from rejecting the principle. So, any definition of omnipotence is inadequate and must be rejected if it entails the claim

From *Philosophical Studies* 32 (1977): 181–90. Reprinted by permission. This paper was written under a 1975 Summer Stipend from the National Endowment for the Humanities.

that an omnipotent being can bring about a state of affairs that is logically impossible to bring about and if any definition of omnipotence is adequate then it does not entail that claim.

Second, it seems reasonable not to expect of an omnipotent being that he be able to bring about a state of affairs that it is logically impossible *for him* to bring about. There is a kind of state of affairs whose description is not self-contradictory and which it is logically possible for some agent or other to bring about but which it is logically impossible for some particular agent to bring about. So, for example, a state of affairs not brought about by an omnipotent being is a state of affairs whose description is not self-contradictory and which it is logically possible for many agents to bring about but which it is logically impossible for an omnipotent being to bring about. It is logically impossible for an omnipotent being to bring about that logically possible state of affairs because to expect of an omnipotent being that he be able to bring about a state of affairs not brought about by an omnipotent being is to expect of an omnipotent being not that he be able to bring about a state of affairs whose description is not self-contradictory but that he be able to bring about a state of affairs whose description is self-contradictory, namely, the state of affairs both brought about and not brought about by an omnipotent being. Accordingly, the claim that an omnipotent being cannot bring about a state of affairs not brought about by an omnipotent being does not entail that the omnipotent being lacks some power or ability and, hence, does not entail that the omnipotent being is not omnipotent. It seems reasonable, then, to adopt the principle that the failure of an omnipotent being to bring about a state of affairs that it is logically impossible for an omnipotent being to bring about does not count against omnipotence or falsify the claim that a being is omnipotent. Clearly, rejecting this principle also leads to logical absurdities. So, any definition of omnipotence is inadequate and must be rejected if it entails the claim that an omnipotent being is able to bring about a state of affairs that it is logically impossible for an omnipotent being to bring about and if any definition of omnipotence is adequate then it does not entail that claim.

Third, it seems reasonable to require of any adequate definition of omnipotence that it be logically compatible with the claims essential to traditional Judaeo-Christian theism concerning the other divine attributes. No definition of omnipotence is compatible with traditional theism which entails that if God is omnipotent then He is not omniscient, not omnipresent, and not all-loving; and no definition of omnipotence which is incompatible with traditional theism in this way is adequate for resolving issues in philosophical theology. Such definitions may indeed provoke philosophical debate, but such debates would be unrelated to the question of the omnipotence of God since these kinds of definitions would entail that the being in question is not the God of traditional theism. So, any definition of omnipotence is inadequate and must be rejected if it entails the claim that if God is omnipotent then He is not omniscient, not omnipresent, and not all-loving; and if any definition of omnipotence is adequate then it does not entail that claim.

Finally, it seems reasonable to demand of any adequate definition of omnipotence that it must not entail that a being is omnipotent who is clearly not omnipotent. Consider, for example, Mr. McEar. Mr. McEar is the man who is capable *only* of scratching his ear[4] and being as impotent as he is it seems intuitively obvious, even in the absence of any adequate criteria for omnipotence, that McEar does not qualify as an omnipotent being. The judgment that McEar is not omnipotent is not based on any definitive definition of omnipotence which McEar fails to satisfy. Rather, the judgment is made preanalytically on the grounds that McEar is the antithesis of what would be acceptable as an omnipotent being. Whatever it is to be an omnipotent being, McEar is not omnipotent because he is almost completely impotent. Accordingly, any definition of omnipotence is vacuous which entails that McEar is omnipotent if he exists. So, any definition of omnipotence is inadequate and must be rejected if it entails the claim that a being is omnipotent who is clearly not omnipotent and if any definition of omnipotence is adequate then it does not entail that claim.

In short, any definition of omnipotence is inadequate and must be rejected if it entails either

(i) That an omnipotent being is able to bring about a state of affairs that it is logically impossible to bring about;

(ii) that an omnipotent being is able to bring about a state of affairs that it is logically impossible for an omnipotent being to bring about;

(iii) that if God is omnipotent then He is not omniscient, not omnipresent, and not all-loving; or

(iv) that a being is omnipotent who is clearly not omnipotent.

Any such definition of omnipotence is inadequate and must be rejected because if it entails (i) or (ii) then it leads to logical absurdities, if it entails (iii) then it is theologically irrelevant, and if it entails (iv) then it is vacuous.

On the other hand, if any definition of omnipotence is adequate then it does not entail any of the statements in (i) through (iv). Notice that the claim here is not that failure to entail any of those statements is a sufficient condition for the adequacy of any definition of omnipotence. It is not being claimed that if any definition of omnipotence does not entail those statements then the definition is adequate. There may well be other statements that any adequate definition of omnipotence must not entail. Rather, the claim here is that failure to entail any of the statements in (i) through (iv) is a *necessary* condition of any adequate definition of omnipotence. It is being claimed that if any definition of omnipotence does entail any of the statements in (i) through (iv) then the definition is not adequate and it must be rejected. So, it is the weaker of these two claims that is being made and this is all that is required in order to show that no adequate definition of omnipotence is possible. For I will now argue that every definition of omnipotence entails either the statement in (iii) or the statement in (iv) and, hence, that every definition of omnipotence is inadequate either because it is theologically irrelevant or because it is vacuous. What I will show is that any definition of omnipotence that is adequate to (iii) [i.e., that *does not* entail (iii)] is inadequate to (iv) [i.e., *does* entail (iv)] and any definition of omnipotence that is adequate to (iv) is inadequate to (iii).

Presumably *any* definition, *D*, of omnipotence will quantify over individuals and states of affairs.[5] So, any such definition *D* will contain an individual variable, say *x*, which ranges over all existent beings and a variable, say *s*, which ranges over all states of affairs. Finally, *D* will make a statement to the effect that with respect to any individual *x* and any state of affairs *s*, the sentence '*x* is omnipotent' equals by definition or is logically equivalent to the sentence 'if *s* satisfies a certain set of conditions *C* then *x* is able to bring about *s*' (where the condition set *C* on *s* is itself logically consistent). Though any such definition *D* may contain other elements as well, this presumably describes the general structure and content minimally necessary to *any* definition, *D*, of omnipotence.

Consider now any definition, *D*, of omnipotence and let us assume that the condition set *C* on *s* of *D* is such that *D* is adequate to (i), (ii), and (iv). That is, we are assuming that the condition set *C* on *s* places conditions on *s* such that *D* does *not* entail either that an omnipotent being is able to bring about a state of affairs that it is logically impossible to bring about, or that an omnipotent being is able to bring about a state of affairs that it is logically impossible for an omnipotent being to bring about, or that a being is omnipotent who is clearly not omnipotent. Furthermore, let us assume that the conditions placed on s by the condition set C are so encompassing that D does not entail that an omnipotent being is able to bring about *any* state of affairs that are in any way problematic *except* that D entails that an omnipotent being is able to bring about

(a) a state of affairs which is such that if it is brought about then it has the property of having been brought about by a single[6] being who has *never at any time* been omniscient,

(b) a state of affairs which is such that if it is brought about then it has the property of having been brought about by a single being who has *never at any time* been omnipresent, and

(c) a state of affairs which is such that if it is brought about then it has the property of having been brought about by a single being who has *never at any time* been all-loving.

That is, we are assuming that the condition set C on s is so complete that D does not entail any statements about what states of affairs an omnipotent being is able to bring about that would in any way require us to reject D except the statements that an omnipotent being is able to bring about the states of affairs mentioned in (a), (b), and (c) above. Since these states of affairs are in no way logically bizarre, our assumption does not require that the condition set C contain any conditions which place logically bizarre restrictions on s in D.

But since D entails that an omnipotent being is able to bring these states of affairs about, D is adequate in every respect *except* that D is not adequate to (iii). Definition D is not adequate to (iii) because if we substitute the proper name 'God' for the individual variable x in D then D entails that if God is omnipotent then He is not now omniscient, not now omnipresent, and not now all-loving. Definition D entails this claim about God because D entails that if God is omnipotent then He is able to bring about the state of affairs mentioned in (a), the state of affairs mentioned in (b), and the state of affairs mentioned in (c). But it is necessarily true that if God is *now* omniscient (omnipresent, all-loving) then every state of affairs that He is *now* able to bring about is such that if He brings it about then it has the property of having been brought about by a being who has at some time or other been omniscient (omnipresent, all-loving). It follows, then, that God is not now omniscient (omnipresent, all-loving) if He is now able to bring about a state of affairs which is such that if He brings it about then it has the property of having been brought about by a (single) being who has never at any time been omniscient (omnipresent, all-loving). So, because D is not adequate to (iii), though it is adequate in every other respect, no such definition, D, of omnipotence is acceptable unless it is made adequate to (iii).

Two procedures are required to make D adequate to (iii). First, it is necessary to locate the source of the problems presented by the states of affairs mentioned in (a) through (c). Second, it is necessary to supplement the condition set C on s or in some other way provide a condition in D which excludes from the required range of x's ability the ability to bring about all those states of affairs having characteristics typical of the problem-causing characteristics found in the states of affairs mentioned in (a) through (c). Notice what problems are presented by the states of affairs mentioned in (a) through (c). The problem presented by (a) is that the occurrence of the state of affairs mentioned in (a) entails[7] that the state of affairs was brought about by a being who has the property of being non-omniscient. The problem presented by (b) is that the occurrence of the state of affairs mentioned in (b) entails that the state of affairs was brought about by a being who has the property of being non-omnipresent. Similarly, the problem presented by (c) is that the occurrence of the state of affairs mentioned in (c) entails that the state of affairs was brought about by a being who has the property of being non-all-loving. It would appear, then, that the source of the problems presented by these states of affairs is the same for each state of affairs. Each one of these states of affairs is such that the occurrence of the state of affairs entails that it was brought about by a being who has a property not possessed by God.

So, in order to make D adequate to (iii) we must in some way place a condition on D which excludes from the required range of x's ability the ability to bring about any state of affairs which is such that the occurrence of the state of affairs entails that it was brought about by a being who has a property not possessed by x. Exactly how this is to be achieved will in all likelihood depend on the individual idiosyncracies of any given formulation of D. One way of doing it, for example, would be to simply add to the condition set C on s a statement something like

(S) The occurrence of s does not entail that s was brought about by a being who has a property not possessed by x.

There are, for all I know, a number of ways to place a condition on *D* which will exclude these unwanted states of affairs from the range of the states of affairs that we expect God to be able to bring about. But, since *D* is *any* definition of omnipotence, *every* adequate definition, *D*, of omnipotence must in some way contain some kind of provision which excludes from the required range of *x*'s ability the ability to bring about this kind of state of affairs. If any definition, *D*, of omnipotence fails to make this kind of provision then *D* will not be adequate to (iii), that is, will entail that if God is omnipotent then He is not omniscient, not omnipresent, and not all-loving. Any such definition, *D*, will be theologically irrelevant and must be rejected.

Let us assume, then, that *D* has been made adequate to (iii) either by adding (S) to the condition set *C* or in some other way. That is, we are assuming that *D* excludes from the required range of *x*'s ability the ability to bring about any state of affairs whose occurrence entails that it was brought about by a being who has a property not possessed by *x*. But, then, any such definition *D* adequate to (iii) is not adequate to (iv), that is, entails that a being is omnipotent who is clearly not omnipotent. For *D* now entails that Mr. McEar, the man who is capable only of scratching his ear, is omnipotent if he exists. It is easy to see why. Consider any state of affairs whatsoever except the scratching of McEar's ear. The occurrence of that state of affairs entails that it was brought about by a being who has a property not possessed by McEar, namely, the property of being able to bring about that state of affairs. So, since McEar does not possess that property, the ability to bring about that state of affairs and the ability to bring about any state of affairs other than the scratchings of his ear is excluded from the required range of McEar's ability when the proper name 'McEar' is substituted for *x* in *D*. Hence, *D* entails that McEar is omnipotent. Indeed, it turns out that everyone is omnipotent by *D*. For given any person and any state of affairs that he is unable to bring about, the occurrence of that state of affairs entails that it was brought about by a being who has a property not possessed by the person, namely, the property of being able to bring about that state of affairs. But, since the person does not possess that property, the ability to bring about that state of affairs and the ability to bring about any other state of affairs that he is unable to bring about is excluded from the required range of his ability when his proper name is substituted for *x* in *D*. So, *D* is not adequate to (iv) because *D* now entails that everyone, including McEar, is omnipotent.

Furthermore, it should be plain that D cannot be made adequate to both (iii) and (iv). For it is just by virtue of which D is adequate to (iii) that it is inadequate to (iv). Definition D is adequate to (iii) because it excludes from the required range of God's ability the ability to bring about any state of affairs whose occurrence entails that it was brought about by a being who has a property not possessed by God. But for every such state of affairs, God has the property of being unable to bring about that state of affairs. Accordingly, D is adequate to (iii) just by virtue of the fact that it excludes from the required range of God's ability the ability to bring about any state of affairs that He is unable to bring about. Put more generally, D is adequate to (iii) just by virtue of the fact that it excludes from the required range of any agent's ability the ability to bring about any state of affairs that the agent is unable to bring about. And it is just by virtue of this fact that D is inadequate to (iv). So, any condition added to D which would make D adequate to (iv) would eliminate this exclusion and would make D inadequate to (iii).

Moreover, D cannot be made adequate to (iv) by adding to the condition set C on s the restriction that

(S1) the description of s does not include any reference to or description of the agent by which s is (to be) brought about.

For while adding (S1) to D would make D adequate to (iii) by excluding from the required range of God's ability the ability to bring about any state of affairs whose occurrence entails that it was brought about by a being who has a property not possessed by God, definition D would still entail that a being is omnipotent who is clearly not omnipotent if he exists. Consider Mr. McChin. Unlike Mr. McEar, Mr. McChin is capable of scratching his own ear as well as his own foot, his own hand, and so on. Indeed, McChin is unlimited in power in a way that satisfies the entire condition set C on s of D, but McChin is a being who is *incapable* of ever scratching anyone's chin. In other words, though McChin is able to bring about any state of affairs prescribed by $D,$ he is unable to bring about any state of affairs in which McChin scratches someone's chin and since every such state of affairs as the latter is one whose description includes a reference to or description of McChin as the agent by which the state of affairs is (to be) brought about, definition D does not require that McChin be able to bring about any such state of affairs in order to be omnipotent when (S1) is added to the condition set C on s of D. So, since McChin is unlimited in power in every respect required by the condition set C on s of D when (S1) is added to C, definition D entails that McChin is omnipotent if he exists. But McChin is clearly not omnipotent since there are an indefinite number of states of affairs that he is unable to bring about, namely, all those states of affairs in which McChin scratches chins. Consequently, (S1) would not make D adequate to (iv) because D would still entail that a being is omnipotent who is clearly not omnipotent. In short, since D is *any* definition of omnipotence, *every* definition of omnipotence adequate to (iii) is inadequate to (iv) and conversely. It follows from this that there is no adequate definition of omnipotence and, hence, that it is impossible to define 'omnipotence.'

What the above argument shows, I think, is that the attempts to provide a *general* definition of omnipotence have been misguided and that the crucial issue for philosophical theology is to try to provide an analysis of what it means to say that *God is omnipotent* or, as Professor Geach[8] prefers to put it, that *God is almighty*. In his own way, Geach rejects the notion of a general definition of omnipotence, which I have now argued is impossible, and provides a discussion which may well point the direction in which future analyses of God's omnipotence ought to go. But whether or not Geach's suggestions point in exactly the right direction, the above argument, if it is correct, shows that some such direction as his is the only profitable one.

NOTES

1. Descartes thought that God could do what is logically impossible, for example, "God cannot have been determined to make it true that contradictions cannot be together, and consequently He could have done the contrary" (letter to Mesland, 2 May 1644). For complete references see Harry G. Frankfurt, "The Logic of Omnipotence," *The Philosophical Review* 73, no. 2 (April 1964): 262–63.

2. Wade Savage, "The Paradox of the Stone," *The Philosophical Review* 76, no. 1 (January 1967): 74–79. On p. 75 Savage suggests that perhaps the claim is admissible that God can do what is self-contradictory. For my part, I find Savage's suggestion incoherent.

3. See note 1 above.

4. As far as I know Alvin Plantinga was the first to use the counterexample of the man who is capable only of scratching his ear. The use occurs in connection with a discussion of omnipotence in *God and Other Minds* (Ithaca, N.Y.: Cornell University Press, 1967), p. 170. I have taken the liberty of baptizing the man "Mr. McEar."

5. This is not quite accurate because D could quantify over actions instead

and be stated in terms of performing actions. The present discussion is stated in terms of states of affairs and bringing them about, but everything that is said and argued in this paper applies *mutatis mutandis* to actions and performing them.

6. By a state of affairs that has been brought about by a *single* being I mean a state of affairs that has been brought about by *one and only one* being as opposed to a state of affairs that has been brought about by two or more beings.

7. Strictly it is not the occurrence of a state of affairs that entails but the *statement* that the state of affairs obtains. However, the finer points of logic sometimes have to yield to considerations of syntax and so I will use the former, less correct, way of speaking instead of the latter, more correct, way of speaking.

8. P. T. Geach, "Omnipotence," *Philosophy* 48, no. 183 (January 1973): 7–20 and "An Irrelevance of Omnipotence," *Philosophy* 48, no. 186 (October 1973): 327–33.

10

The Hidden Assumption
in the Paradox of Omnipotence

The paradox of omnipotence is commonly cited by the atheologian in order to pose a problem for the theologian. It is intended to show the theologian that he cannot maintain the doctrine of divine omnipotence. The paradox is stated as a dilemma and can be formulated as follows:

(1) Either God can create a stone that He cannot lift or God cannot create a stone that He cannot lift.

(2) If God can create a stone that He cannot lift, then it is possible that there be something God cannot do, namely, lift a certain stone. But, then, if it is possible that there be a stone that God cannot lift, God is not omnipotent.

(3) If God cannot create a stone that He cannot lift, then there is already something God cannot do, namely, create the stone in question. But, then, if God cannot create a stone that He cannot lift, God is not omnipotent.

(4) Therefore, God is not omnipotent.

But notice, now, that the first horn of the dilemma assumes that being omnipotent entails being able to lift anything and the second horn of the dilemma assumes that being omnipotent entails being able to create any-

From *Philosophy and Phenomenological Research* 38, no. 1 (September 1977): 125–27. Reprinted by permission. This paper was written under a 1975 Summer Stipend from the National Endowment for the Humanities.

thing. In other words, the dilemma posed by the atheologian rests on the assumption

(A) '*x* is omnipotent' entails '*x* can lift anything and *x* can create anything.'

However, once assumption (A) of the dilemma is made explicit, the theologian need not be bothered by the dilemma nor does the dilemma require him to abandon the doctrine of divine omnipotence because the theologian is not required by either logic or doctrine to subscribe to assumption (A) upon which the dilemma rests. Indeed, the theologian can consistently reject (A). Notice that (A) entails that any true statement of the form 'God cannot create O' counts against or falsifies the claim that God is omnipotent. But the theologian need not agree that any true statement of that form counts against divine omnipotence. The theologian can maintain, for example, that the statement 'God cannot create a round square' does not count against the omnipotence of God because the statement 'God created a round square' entails that there is an object all of whose properties are such that the statement that the object has those properties entails a contradiction. So, the theologian can maintain, since the failure to create what is logically impossible does not count against the omnipotence of God, the statement, 'God cannot create a round square,' does not falsify the claim that God is omnipotent. Accordingly, the theologian can consistently hold that it is false that any true statement of the form, 'God cannot create O,' counts against divine omnipotence and, hence, he can maintain that the assumption (A) is false. But, then, since the dilemma rests on assumption (A) and since assumption (A) is false, the dilemma does not provide a problem for the theologian.

Perhaps, though, the atheologian's original claim against the theologian can be sustained if we reformulate (A). The problem with (A) is that it entails that an omnipotent being can create such objects as round squares. So, if we can reformulate (A) in such a way as to exclude such objects as round squares from the creative scope of an omnipotent being, then perhaps the theologian will have to abandon the doctrine of divine omnipotence after all. One way to effect this change that immediately suggests itself is to replace (A) with something like

(A') '*x* is omnipotent' entails '*x* can lift anything and *x* can create anything whose description is not self-contradictory.'

The substitute, (A'), would seem to be free from the problem which (A) had because (A') does not entail that the statement, 'God cannot create round squares,' falsifies the claim that God is omnipotent. However, whether or not the theologian is willing to accept (A'), (A') will not sustain the atheologian's original claim against the theologian because the dilemma will not go through with (A'). Notice that (A') entails that everything created by God will have the property of being created by a being who can lift anything. So any stone created by God will have the property of being liftable by God. But then (A') does *not* entail that the statement, 'God cannot create a stone that He cannot lift,' falsifies the claim that God is omnipotent because the statement, 'God created a stone that He cannot lift,' entails that there is a stone which has both the property of being liftable by God and the property of being unliftable by God, that is, entails that there is an object all of whose properties are such that the statement that the object has those properties entails a contradiction.[1] Furthermore, since the failure to create what is logically impossible *does not* count against the omnipotence of God, the statement, 'God cannot create a stone that He cannot lift,' does *in fact not* falsify the claim that God is omnipotent. So (A') does not sustain the second horn of the dilemma, and consequently the dilemma does not go through. In short, the substitute (A') does not require that the theologian abandon the doctrine of divine omnipotence.

It turns out then that in citing the paradox of omnipotence either the atheologian will assume something like (A) or the atheologian will assume something like (A'). If the atheologian assumes something like (A), then the theologian has no problem. If the atheologian assumes something like (A'), then the theologian has no problem. Therefore, when the atheologian cites the paradox of omnipotence, the theologian has no problem.

NOTE

1. Bernard Mayo and George Mavrodes have claimed that a stone too heavy for God to lift is on a logical par with a round square, but they have not made clear either that the dilemma assumes a specific and exceptionable concept of omnipotence or how their claim relates explicitly to the assumption or the dilemma itself for showing that the dilemma does not go through. See Bernard Mayo, "Mr. Keene on Omnipotence," *Mind* 70, no. 278 (April 1961): 249–50; and George Mavrodes, "Some Puzzles Concerning Omnipotence," *Philosophical Review* 72 (1963): 221–23.

11

Augustine on the Simplicity of God

Almost all of the claims about the nature or essence of God that are made by Augustine and other theists in the tradition of Judaeo-Christian monotheism have been thought by one philosopher or another to be either puzzling or problematic at the very least or paradoxical or downright self-contradictory at the very worst. For example, the set of claims that God is omnibenevolent, that God is omniscient, that God is omnipotent, and that evil exists, has been regarded by many philosophers as problematic for the theist if not actually self-contradictory and the claim itself that God is omnipotent has been regarded by many philosophers as paradoxical if not actually self-contradictory. All of the claims about the nature or essence of God that are shared by both Augustine and other traditional theists have at least two features in common. First, all such claims are essential to the integrity of both Augustine's theology and the theology of orthodox theism. Second, each one of these claims is intended to characterize God as absolutely different in some respect from everything else. For example, the claim that God is the creator of everything, that every item in the realm of reality is without exception either something that belongs to the Divine nature or something that was made by the Divine nature, is essential to Augustine's theology as well as to the theology of orthodox theism and that claim is intended to characterize God as absolutely

From *The New Scholasticism* 51, no. 4 (Autumn 1977): 453–68. Reprinted by permission. This paper was written under a Faculty Research Fellowship for 1976 from the Research Foundation of the State University of New York.

distinguishable from every other thing by virtue of the fact that He alone is an uncreated nature while every other thing is without exception a created nature. As with almost every other claim about the nature or essence of God, the claim that God is the uncreated creator of everything has not been overlooked by the critics of traditional theism.

Perhaps one of the most puzzling claims about God's nature or essence, and one that has been for the most part ignored by the critics of orthodox theism, is the claim that God is simple, that God is absolutely distinguishable from every other thing by virtue of the fact that He alone is simple while every other nature is without exception manifold. This claim is puzzling and the reason that the puzzle has been almost entirely ignored by the critics of theism is that the claim is usually made by the theist in a context which generates problems far more obvious than the ones that are generated solely by the claim that God is simple. As it is in the works of Augustine, the claim that God is simple is usually made by the theist in connection with the claim that God is a trinity of persons. Given the mind-boggling problems generated by the grosser claim that God's nature is at once both simple and tripartite, it is not at all surprising that a critic might overlook the more subtle difficulties lurking behind the claim that God is simple in favor of sorting out the entailments and problems involved in the claim that God is by nature a simple trinity. Though the difficulties involved in the puzzle of Divine simplicity are more subtle than the difficulties involved in the puzzle of the Divine trinity, the former difficulties are no less problematic and no less important than the latter. What is puzzling about the claim that God is simple is that it is not at all clear just what there is about God that distinguishes Him from every other nature when He is said to be simple and they are said to be manifold, and so it is not at all clear that the claim about God's simplicity is correct nor is it even clear that there is any explication or analysis of the distinction between what is simple and what is manifold that would make it manifest that the distinction is indeed a coherent one. It is not possible here to examine every available account of the doctrine of Divine simplicity, but perhaps an examination of Augustine's account will show us whether or not he has contributed anything to the discussion of that doctrine that would advance our understanding of the concept of Divine simplicity.

As far as I am able to determine, Chapter 10 of Book XI in *The City of God* is the single most detailed account of the doctrine of God's simplicity given by Augustine, but in spite of the detail of the account Augustine provides there, that account is none the less puzzling. For, in what would appear to be the most informative statement of the concept of simplicity that occurs in this passage, Augustine tells us that "a nature is said to be simple on the grounds that it cannot lose any of the properties that it possesses; that is, there is no distinction to be made between what that nature is and the properties that it has" (my translation of "propter hoc itaque natura dicitur simplex, cui non sit aliquid habere quod vel possit amittere; vel aliud sit habens, aliud quod habet"). In order to lay out what is puzzling about this statement of the concept of simplicity I shall construe the use of the word 'property' in this context in such a way that a thing, x, has the property of being P (the property of being a P) if and only if the statement that x is P (that x is a P) is true. A thing, x, will be said to have the property of being P at a given time t if and only if the statement that x is P at t (that x is a P at t) is true. I shall also distinguish between contingent properties and necessary properties. A property, P, will be said to be a *contingent* property with respect to a thing, x, if and only if x can begin to possess P or cease to possess P. A property, P, will be said to be a *necessary* property with respect to a thing, x, if and only if x possesses P and x cannot begin to possess P or cease to possess P, that is, if and only if x has P but P is not a contingent property with respect to x. In other words, a property is contingent with respect to something just in case it is possible that the thing have the property at one time and fail to have it at another time, and a property is necessary with respect to something just in case it is impossible that the thing have the property at one time and fail to have it at another time. By this distinction the property of being yellow is a contingent property of a yellow book because the property of being yellow is a property that a book can begin to possess and cease to possess. On the other hand, the property of being extended in space and time is a necessary property of a yellow book because that property is one that a yellow book possesses and it is one that a yellow book cannot begin to possess or cease to possess.

With this understanding of the concepts of property, contingent property, and necessary property it might reasonably be supposed that Augustine's account of what constitutes a simple nature is to be understood as the claim that a thing, x, is simple if and only if x does not have any contingent properties, for Augustine claims that a nature is simple by virtue of the fact that it cannot lose any of the properties that it possesses. But on this understanding of Augustine's account of the concept of simplicity it seems quite plain that God is not simple because the statement that

God was rejected by Augustine in 371 is true while the statement that God was rejected by Augustine in 387 is false. So God had a property at one time (the property of being rejected by Augustine) that He did not have at another time and it is quite apparent that God has an indefinitely large number of such properties. This obvious fact alone makes Augustine's account of the concept of simplicity puzzling for he himself acknowledges that God has such properties. In Chapter 16 of Book V in the *De Trinitate* Augustine says that there was a time at which God began to possess the property of being the Lord of the people of Israel for if God had this property from eternity then we would be compelled to admit that the people of Israel have existed from eternity. So, under the present understanding of Augustine's account of simplicity God is *not* simple and God is *not* in fact distinguishable from every other thing by virtue of the fact that He alone has no contingent properties while every other nature does without exception have contingent properties, for God also has contingent properties.

However, it might be that this understanding of Augustine's account of simplicity is incorrect. Perhaps when he says that a simple nature cannot lose any of the properties it possesses, he does *not* mean that it has no contingent properties. Instead he may mean that a simple nature is the kind of thing that need not have any contingent properties, even though it might have some as a matter of fact, while a manifold nature on the other hand is the kind of thing that must have contingent properties. It may be that Augustine thinks that God is absolutely distinguishable from every other thing by virtue of the fact that He alone need not have any contingent properties while every other nature must without exception have contingent properties. So it may be that Augustine's account of what constitutes a simple nature is to be understood as the claim that a thing, *x,* is simple if and only if it is possible for *x* not to possess any contingent properties. On this understanding of the doctrine of simplicity, God would be absolutely unique by virtue of the fact that He is the only thing that could exist with all and only necessary properties. All other things would without exception be distinct from God by virtue of the fact that they can exist only if they have contingent properties.

But this second explanation of Augustine's account of simplicity is no better than the first one. A doctrine quite clearly essential to Augustine's theology and to the theology of orthodox theism is the doctrine that being omniscient is a property that God has necessarily, that is, that omniscience is not a property that God can have at one time and not have at another time. On Augustine's view and on the view of all traditional theists, God has the property of being omniscient and the property of being omniscient is not a property that God can fail to possess. However, on this second understanding of Augustine's account of the concept of simplicity the doctrine that God is simple turns out to be logically incompatible with the doctrine that omniscience is a necessary property of God, and it is fairly easy to see why. The statement that there are dinosaurs is obviously a contingent statement; that is, although the statement is false it might very well have been true. On the same grounds the statement that there are no dinosaurs is also a contingent statement, although it is true it might very well have been false. So the property of knowing that there are dinosaurs *and* the property of knowing that there are no dinosaurs are *both* contingent properties with respect to *every* individual. This is so because which one of these two properties an individual happens to have depends on which one of two distinct contingent states of affairs happens to obtain, for it depends on whether or not there happen to be any dinosaurs. If there are dinosaurs then one can have the property of knowing that there are dinosaurs, but no one can have the property of knowing that there are no dinosaurs; and if there are no dinosaurs then one can have the property of knowing that there are no dinosaurs, but no one can have the property of knowing that there are dinosaurs. So if there are dinosaurs and God has the property of being omniscient then God has the contingent property of knowing that there are dinosaurs, and if there are no dinosaurs and God has the property of being omniscient then God has the contingent property of knowing that there are no dinosaurs.

Now, since it is necessarily true that either there are dinosaurs or there are no dinosaurs and since omniscience is a necessary property of God, it is necessary that God has either the property of knowing that there are dinosaurs or the property of knowing that there are no dinosaurs. And since both of these properties are contingent properties with respect to God it follows that God necessarily has one or the other of two contingent properties. In other words, it cannot at any time be true of God that He has neither the one nor the other of these two contingent properties and so it is a necessary property of God that He have at least one contingent property, if the property of being omniscient is one of His necessary properties. On this second understanding of Augustine's account of the concept of simplicity, God cannot have both the property of being simple and the property of being necessarily omniscient as well, and so this second understanding of Augustine's account of simplicity fares no better than the first one. If God has the property of being necessarily omniscient, then God is *not* simple and God is *not* distinguishable from every other thing by virtue of the fact that He alone need not have any contingent properties while every other nature must without exception have contingent properties, for God like everything else must also have contingent properties.[1]

So far there does not seem to be any explication of Augustine's account of the concept of simplicity which would make it possible to describe a difference that actually exists between God and every other thing. Yet Augustine seems to think there is a real difference between God and every other thing and that his account of the concept of simplicity makes it possible to describe the difference which actually exists between them by saying that God *cannot* lose any of the properties that He possesses while every other thing *can* lose some of the properties that it possesses. If Augustine is correct in his account of the concept of simplicity and if that account makes it possible to describe a difference which really exists between God and every other thing, then his account of the concept of simplicity and the distinction it makes possible cannot be explicated solely in terms of whether or not God and every other thing have contingent properties because the discussion up to this point has shown that God like every other thing has contingent properties and that God like every thing *must* have contingent properties. If Augustine is correct and if his account of simplicity and the distinction made possible by it can be explicated by reference to contingent properties even though they cannot be explicated solely in terms of whether or not God and every other thing has contingent properties, then the difference between God and every other thing must be a difference between the kind of properties that are contingent for God and the kind of properties that are contingent for every other thing.

Augustine seems to be suggesting something very much like this in Chapter 16 of Book V in the *De Trinitate*. There he says that although the property of being the Lord of the people of Israel is a contingent property with respect to God its being contingent does not pose any problems for the doctrine that God is unchangeable. No problems arise for that doctrine because the property of being the Lord of the people of Israel is, as he puts it, *relative* and when God begins to have that property "nothing happens to His nature by which He may be changed."[2] Augustine explains this claim by saying that the property of being a friend to someone is also a contingent property that is relative, but when a person begins to have *this* property something happens to his will by which a change occurs in his nature. What happens is that the person also begins to have the property of being a loving person. So when a person begins to have the relative contingent property of being a friend to someone he also begins to have a second and distinct contingent property that is *not* relative, namely, the property of being a loving person. On the other hand, when that which we call 'money' begins to have or ceases to have the relative contingent property of being a price for something, it does not undergo any change because it does not thereby begin to have or cease to have some further contingent property. Likewise, when God begins to have the relative contingent property of being the Lord of the people of Israel there is no change in His nature because He does not begin to possess or cease to possess some additional contingent property. So that which we call 'money' remains the same when it begins to have or ceases to have the relative contingent property of being a price for something, and God remains exactly the same when He begins to have or ceases to have the relative contingent property of being the Lord of the people of Israel, but a person does not remain the same when he begins to have or ceases to have the relative contingent property of being a friend to someone, because he also begins to have or ceases to have the *non*relative contingent property of being a loving person as a result.

If my understanding of Augustine is correct he is making two crucial distinctions in this passage and in other passages in Book V of the *De Trinitate* as well. First, he is making a distinction between relative properties and nonrelative properties. Second, he is making a distinction between beginning to have or ceasing to have relative properties and beginning to have or ceasing to have nonrelative properties; that is, he is making a distinction between relative contingent properties and nonrelative contingent properties. By employing these distinctions he also explicates what he means by saying that a change occurs in something. On Augustine's view change in a subject does *not* consist in its beginning to have or ceasing to have a relative property; instead change in a subject consists in its beginning to have or ceasing to have a *non*relative property. So for Augustine a nature changes if and only if it begins to have or ceases to have some nonrelative property. On the basis of this explication of change a thing can be said to be subject to change or capable of change if it can begin to possess or cease to possess a property that is nonrelative; that is, a thing is subject to change if it has nonrelative properties that are also contingent. Augustine's main point in this passage appears to be that God is not subject to or capable of change and the fact that He has the property of being the Lord of the people of Israel at one time and not at another time does not falsify the claim that He is absolutely unchangeable. That fact does not falsify that claim because the contingent property of being the Lord of the people of Israel is a *relative* property and the fact that God has it at one time and not at another time does not entail that He has any *nonrelative* properties that He can have at one time and not at another time; that is, it does not entail that God has any nonrelative properties that are also contingent. On the other hand, a finite person *is* subject to change, and the fact that such a person *can* have the property of being a friend to someone at one time, and not at another time, *does* falsify the claim that the person is unchangeable. That fact falsifies that claim because while the contingent property of being a friend to someone is also a relative property the fact that the person can have it at one time and not at another time does entail that he has a nonrelative property that he can have at one time and not at another time; that is, it entails that he has a nonrelative property that is also contingent. So Augustine's view appears to be that God is unchangeable by virtue of the fact that He does not have any nonrelative properties that are contingent and that every other thing is changeable by virtue of the fact that it has nonrelative properties that are contingent.

Perhaps we are now making some progress in our attempt to achieve a clear understanding of Augustine's account of the concept of simplicity. For in *The City of God,* in the same chapter (XI, 10) that contains the account of the concept of simplicity which we are now considering, Augustine also says that God is simple and therefore unchangeable and that every other thing is not simple and therefore not unchangeable. This claim makes it apparent that Augustine holds the view that a thing is simple if and only if it is unchangeable. So, since a thing is unchangeable on his view if and only if it cannot begin to have or cease to have any of its nonrelative properties, it might very well be that when Augustine says that a simple nature cannot lose any of the properties that it possesses he means that a simple nature cannot lose any of its nonrelative properties. Given his view that a thing is simple if and only if it is unchangeable, it might reasonably be supposed that Augustine's account of the concept of simplicity is to be understood as the claim that a thing, *x,* is simple if and only if *x* does not have any nonrelative properties that are contingent (or if and only if all of the contingent properties possessed by *x* are relative). On this understanding of Augustine's account of the concept of simplicity God would presumably be absolutely distinguishable from every other thing by virtue of the fact that He alone does not have any nonrelative properties that are contingent while every other thing does without exception have nonrelative properties that are contingent.

But this third understanding of Augustine's account of the concept of simplicity does not appear to be a great deal clearer than the first two. For while it may be possible to get a vague intuitive idea of what Augustine has in mind when he talks about the difference between relative properties and nonrelative properties, he does not provide any explicit formulation of that distinction which would make it possible to decide for any given property whatsoever whether it is a relative property or a nonrelative property, and so it is not unexceptionably clear just exactly what the difference is that is supposed to obtain between relative properties and nonrelative properties. Nevertheless, even though Augustine does not provide any explicit statement of the difference he believes to obtain between relative properties and nonrelative properties, it may be possible to construct a coherent and acceptable formulation of that distinction from what he does say about it.

In Chapter 8 of Book V in the *De Trinitate* Augustine says we should hold fast above all to the principle that "whatever in that divine and exalted sublimity is said in reference to Himself is said according to the substance; but what is said in reference to something does not refer to a substance but to a relationship."[3] Here it seems that Augustine is talking about nonrelative predication on the one hand and relative predication on the other. What he appears to be saying is that whenever we talk about God either we are saying something about the way He stands in relation to Himself or we are saying something about the way He stands in relation to something other than Himself. Perhaps what Augustine wants us to notice here is that in a statement of nonrelative predication about God the statement does not refer to any being other than God while in a statement of relative predication about God the statement refers not only to God but also to another being distinct from God. If this is what Augustine has in mind then he may want to suggest the more general claim that a property is relative with respect to a subject just in case the predication statement (i.e., the statement that the subject has the property) refers to a being not identical to the subject. On this account the property of being the Lord of the people of Israel would be a *relative* property with respect to God because the statement that God has the property of being the Lord of the people of Israel does refer to beings not identical to God and the property of being omniscient would be a *non*relative property with respect to God because the statement that God has the property of being omniscient does *not* refer to a being not identical to God. So far this present suggestion looks quite promising for from an intuitive point of view we would expect these two properties to turn out to be relative and nonrelative respectively. If this is indeed what Augustine wants to suggest in this passage from Chapter 8 then it would seem that his distinction between relative properties and nonrelative properties can be formulated by saying that for any property, *P,* and for anything, *x,*

(1) *P* is relative with respect to *x* if and only if '*x* has *P*' is a statement that refers to a being not identical to *x,*

adding, of course, that a property is *nonrelative* with respect to a subject just in case the subject has the property but the property is not relative with respect to the subject.

However, (1) will not do as an acceptable formulation of the distinction between relative properties and nonrelative properties. Consider the property of being omniscient and the entity worshipped by Augustine. By (1) the property of being omniscient is a relative property with respect to the entity worshipped by Augustine because the statement *the entity worshipped by Augustine has the property of being omniscient* does refer to a being not identical to the entity worshipped by Augustine. That statement refers to Augustine, who is quite clearly not identical to the entity worshipped by Augustine. All of the available evidence indicates that the entity worshipped by Augustine is God and so by (1) the property of being omniscient is a relative property with respect to God because it is a relative property with respect to the entity worshipped by Augustine. But it has already been shown that by (1) the property of being omniscient is a nonrelative property with respect to God and so it turns out that (1) entails that the property of being omniscient is both a relative property and a nonrelative property with respect to God; that is, it turns out that (1) entails a contradiction. Because any statement is incoherent if it entails a contradiction, (1) is not an acceptable formulation of the distinction between relative properties and nonrelative properties and so it must be rejected.

Perhaps, though, it is possible to construct a formulation of Augustine's distinction which is not subject to the difficulty that was found for (1). The problem with (1) arose because it is possible to denote the subject of a statement by using a definite description that refers to a being not identical to the subject of the statement. But it is not the subject of a statement that ascribes the possession of a property to the subject of the statement; rather it is the predicate of a statement that ascribes the possession of a property to the subject of the statement. So perhaps Augustine would suggest that it is the predicate of a statement that determines whether or not a property is relative. He might want to suggest that if the predicate of a statement refers to a being not identical to the subject of the statement then the property ascribed in that predicate is a relative property, whereas if the predicate of a statement does not refer to a being not identical to the subject of the statement then the property ascribed in that predicate is a nonrelative property. If this or something like it is what Augustine has in mind then it is possible to replace (1) with

(2) *P* is relative with respect to *x* if and only if '*x* has *P*' is a statement containing a predicate that refers to a being not identical to *x*.

Given (2), the property of being omniscient is now a nonrelative property for *both* God *and* the entity worshipped by Augustine, for the predicate 'has the property of being omniscient' is a predicate that does not refer to a being not identical to God nor does it refer to a being not identical to the entity worshipped by Augustine. So (2) appears to escape the problem that prevents the adoption of (1).

Even so, (2) is not acceptable either, because it is subject to a different but similar difficulty. Consider *the property I am thinking of* and suppose that I am thinking of the property of being omniscient. Quite clearly it is true that God has the property I am thinking of if and only if it is true that He has the property of being omniscient. So if God does have the property of being omniscient as Augustine would have us believe, then God has the property I am thinking of. But since the predicate 'has the property I am thinking of' is a predicate that does refer to a being not identical to God, it follows from (2) that the property I am thinking of is a relative property with respect to God; and since the property I am thinking of is the property of being omniscient, then the property of being omniscient is a relative property with respect to God. However, it has already been shown that by (2) the property of being omniscient is a nonrelative property with respect to God and so it turns out that (2) entails that the property of being omniscient is both a relative property and a nonrelative property with respect to God; that is, it turns out that (2) entails a contradiction. The result is that (2) is also incoherent and must be rejected as an acceptable formulation of the distinction between relative properties and nonrelative properties.

The problem with (2) is quite clearly an analogue of the problem with (1). The difficulty which arose for (1) was that it is possible to denote the *subject* of a statement intended to be a statement of nonrelative predication by using a definite description which refers to a being not identical to the subject of that statement. The difficulty which arises for (2) is that it is possible to denote the *predicate* of a statement intended to be a statement of nonrelative predication by using a definite description which refers to a being not identical to the subject of that statement. But while the problem with (2) is an analogue of the problem with (1), it is quite plain that there is no way of escaping the problem with (2) that is an analogue of the way of escaping the problem with (1). No way of this kind is open for escaping the problem with (2) because the basic principle with which Augustine seems to be operating here is the principle that a property is relative just in case a term denoting the property occurs in a statement of predication and the statement in some way refers to a being not identical to the subject of that statement. But reference of this kind could be made in a statement of predication only by either the subject of the statement or the predicate of the statement. So having formulated (2) by eliminating the subject term of a statement of relative predication as the allowable referring term in that statement, it is not now possible to place the same restrictions on the predicate term of that statement as well, and thus the problem that arises for (2) cannot be overcome by eliminating the predicate term as the allowable referring term in a statement of relative predication. Even if (2) were to be reformulated by eliminating the concept 'referring to' and replacing it with some other concept like 'entailing the existence of' or 'asserting something about,' it would still not be possible to produce a statement of the distinction between relative properties and nonrelative properties that overcomes the problem with (2). For, the statement that God has the property of being the Lord of the people of Israel and the statement that God has the property I am thinking of, *both* entail the existence of a being not identical to the subject of the statement; and if the first statement can properly be said to assert something about a being not identical to the subject of the statement (namely, that the people of Israel have the property of being the subjects of God), then the second statement can properly be said to assert something about a being not identical to the subject of the statement (namely, that I have the property of thinking about a property of God). In short, because there is no difference of a logical kind between the property I am thinking of and the property of being the Lord of the people of Israel, it is not possible to produce a formulation of the distinction between relative properties and nonrelative properties that will escape the problem with (2) and so any formulation of that distinction will be incoherent, as is (2).

The result is that Augustine's distinction between relative properties and nonrelative properties is incoherent. Consequently, his account of the concept of unchangeableness is also incoherent, and if the third understanding of his account of the concept of simplicity is correct then his account of the concept of simplicity is incoherent as well. These accounts are incoherent because Augustine's claim that a nature is unchangeable and the third understanding of his claim that a nature is simple are both defined in terms of the distinction between relative properties and nonrelative properties. On the other hand, if the third understanding of Augustine's account of the concept of simplicity is not correct then there remains the puzzle of wondering just exactly what he did mean by the claim that a simple nature cannot lose any of the properties that it possesses, for he does not appear to have supplied any further hints for understanding that claim. In any case, either Augustine's account of the concept of simplicity is incoherent like his account of the concept of unchangeableness, or else Augustine has presented a puzzle without providing any hints for finding a solution to that puzzle.[4]

NOTES

1. The statement that God might not have had any contingent properties itself seems a bit paradoxical for it suggests that it is only contingent that God has any contingent properties and, hence, that God would have at least one contingent property even if He had no contingent properties.

2. Augustine, *The Trinity,* trans. by Stephen McKenna, The Fathers of the Church (Washington, D.C., 1963), p. 196.

3. Ibid., p. 185.

4. For a discussion related to some of the issues considered in this paper see Alvin Plantinga, *God and Other Minds* (Ithaca, N.Y.: Cornell University Press, 1967), pp. 173–80; James Tomberlin, "Plantinga's Puzzles About God and Other Minds," *The Philosophical Forum* 1, no. 3 (Spring 1969, New Series): 365–91 and "Omniscience and Necessity: Putting Humpty-Dumpty Together Again," *The Philosophical Forum* 2, no. 1 (Fall 1970, New Series): 149–51; and Richard La Croix, "God Might Not Love Us," *International Journal for Philosophy of Religion* 5, no. 3 (Fall 1974): 157–61.

12

Failing to Define 'Omnipotence'

Recently in this Journal I argued that it is impossible to produce a satisfactory definition of 'omnipotence' which universally generalizes over persons because any such definition will entail either that a being is omnipotent who is clearly not omnipotent or that if God is omnipotent then he is not omniscient, not omnipresent, and not all-loving.[1] In the same issue George Mavrodes claims to have refuted my argument by producing a definition which he thinks does not entail either of those undesirable results. Unfortunately his definition fails for just the reasons I cited in my original argument. It fails because there are two problems with his second condition, (C2), which is intended to rule out certain propositions from those which a being must be able to satisfy to qualify as omnipotent. Specifically it is intended to rule out: (4) A non-omnipotent being brings it about that Hidden Valley is flooded, and no omnipotent being brings it about that Hidden Valley is flooded.

The first problem is with the antecedent condition of (C2) because it is not clear what Mavrodes means by saying that some proposition, p, entails that some proposition, q, *is satisfied*. What he says is that "a state of affairs, S, *satisfies* a proposition, p, if and only if p could not fail to be true if S were actually to obtain." So, presumably a proposition, q, *is satisfied* if and only if there is some state of affairs, S, which actually

From *Philosophical Studies* 34 (1978): 219–22. Reprinted by permission. This paper was written under a Faculty Research Fellowship for 1977 from the Research Foundation of the State University of New York.

does obtain such that 'S actually obtains' entails 'q is true.' Accordingly, a proposition, p, entails that some proposition, q, *is satisfied* if and only if p entails that there is some proposition, q, and some state of affairs, S, such that 'S actually obtains' entails 'q is true.'

The second problem is with the consequent condition of (C2) because it is not clear what the condition is under which a proposition is properly said to *exclude* an agent or class of agents from among those which may have brought about a given state of affairs and Mavrodes does not say. In spite of this omission (4) suggests what that condition is. Quite clearly (4) *states* or *asserts* that no omnipotent being brought about the state of affairs in question. Presumably what Mavrodes has in mind is that (C2) is to be read as: (C2a) if p entails that there is some proposition, q, and some state of affairs, S, such that 'S actually obtains' entails 'q is true,' and if it is not a necessary truth that no agent can have brought about S, then p does not *state* or *assert* that any agent, or class of agents, is not among those which may have brought about S.

It turns out that Mavrodes is correct in claiming that his definition rules out his own example (4) from the set of propositions a being must be able to satisfy to qualify as omnipotent. But consider a different example: (4a) Hidden Valley is flooded and that flooding of Hidden Valley is brought about by a *single* being[2] who is never at any time omniscient (omnipresent, all-loving). Now, (4a) meets the antecedent conditions of (C2a), but it also meets the consequent condition because (4a) does *not* state or assert that any agent or class of agents is not among those which may have brought about the flooding of Hidden Valley by a single being who is never at any time omniscient (omnipresent, all-loving). Hence (C2a) does not rule out (4a) from those propositions a being must be able to satisfy in order to qualify as omnipotent.

So, Mavrodes' definition entails that an omnipotent being is able to bring about the flooding of Hidden Valley by a single being who is never at any time omniscient (omnipresent, all-loving). And if an omnipotent being is able to bring about that state of affairs, then he is able to bring about a state of affairs which is such that if it is brought about then it has the property of having been brought about by a single being who is never at any time omniscient (omnipresent, all-loving). Consequently, Mavrodes' definition entails that if God is omnipotent then he is not omniscient, not omnipresent, and not all-loving,[3] and it fails to refute my argument because it entails exactly what my argument claimed it would entail.

Perhaps Mavrodes would now amend (C2a), for (4a) entails: (4b) There is a flooding of Hidden Valley and no being who is ever at any time omniscient (omnipresent, all-loving) brought about that flooding of Hidden Valley. And (4b) *does* state or assert that a class of agents is not among those which may have brought about the state of affairs in question. Accordingly, Mavrodes could revise the consequent condition of (C2a) and replace (C2a) with: (C2b) . . . , then *p* does not entail any proposition, *r*, which states or asserts that any agent, or class of agents, is not among those which may have brought about *S*. Since (4a) entails (4b), (C2b) would rule out (4a) and the definition would no longer entail that if God is omnipotent then he is not omniscient, not omnipresent, and not all-loving. But the result of this revision would be that his definition would now entail that a being is omnipotent who is clearly not omnipotent, and this is just the result I argued would occur when such a definition is revised to overcome the former difficulty. To see this consider two propositions that Mavrodes claims are *not* ruled out by his definition. They are: (0) China is invaded by a Swiss army; and (1) Hidden Valley is flooded. Both propositions meet the antecedent conditions of (C2b), but they *fail* to meet the consequent condition of (C2b) because each entails a proposition which states or asserts that a class of agents is not among those which may have brought about the requisite state of affairs. Proposition (0) entails: (0a) There is an invading of China by a Swiss army and no being who is unable to bring about any invading of China brought about that invading of China. Proposition (1) entails: (1a) There is a flooding of Hidden Valley and no being who is unable to bring about any flooding of Hidden Valley brought about that flooding of Hidden Valley. Since both (0) and (1) fail to meet the consequent condition of (C2b), Mavrodes' definition, were it to include (C2b) instead of (C2a), would rule out both (0) and (1) from the set of propositions a being must be able to satisfy to qualify as omnipotent and so a being would qualify as omnipotent on his definition who is clearly not omnipotent.

Moreover, just as (0) entails (0a) and (1) entails (1a), every proposition, *p*, entails some proposition, *r*, which states or asserts that a class of agents is not among those which may have brought about some requisite state of affairs. This is so because it is necessarily true that for any given state of affairs, *S*, no being who is unable to bring about any *S*-kind state of affairs brought about *S*. So, (C2b) rules out every proposition from the set of propositions a being must be able to satisfy in order to qualify as omnipotent. It turns out that if Mavrodes were to amend his definition by substituting (C2b) for (C2a), then the class of propositions over which his definition would range is empty and, hence, his definition would entail that everyone is omnipotent. In short, Mavrodes' definition entails either one or the other of two unacceptable propositions as I argued would be the case for any general definition of 'omnipotence' and so his definition fails to refute my argument.

NOTES

1. "The Impossibility of Defining 'Omnipotence,' "*Philosophical Studies* 32 (1977): 181–90.

2. By a state of affairs that is brought about by a *single* being I mean a state of affairs that is brought about by *one and only one* being as opposed to a state of affairs that is brought about by two or more beings.

3. For a more detailed account of the principles by which this follows from the preceding sentences see "The Impossibility of Defining 'Omnipotence.' "

13

Is There a Paradox of Omniscience?

In a 1965 article,[1] J. L. Cowan makes several provocative claims. The central claim is that he has produced an argument which shows that the paradox of omnipotence scuttles the doctrine of divine omnipotence. A secondary but equally important claim is that he has discovered a paradox of omniscience which scuttles the doctrine of divine omniscience. Except for the meager statement: "The same argument, moreover, is applicable to other omniconcepts. It is applicable, for example, to omniscience. Does God know how to create a universe the potentialities of which he does not know?"[2] Cowan neither formulates the paradox of omniscience, nor gives us directions for applying his argument on the paradox of omnipotence to it. His claims about omniscience are interesting but not at all obvious. Perhaps it will be possible to discover how the paradox of omniscience is to be formulated and to understand what recipe Cowan has in mind for applying his argument to the paradox of omniscience if we outline and examine what he has to say about the paradox of omnipotence.

Cowan accepts the principle that God's inability to do anything the description of which is self-contradictory does not provide a valid objection to the doctrine that God can do anything. However, Cowan insists that there are predicates which are not self-contradictory and which yet raise difficulties for the concept of omnipotence, for example, "making something

From *The Modern Schoolman* 56, no. 3 (March 1979): 251–65. Reprinted by permission. This paper was written under a 1975 Summer Stipend from the National Endowment for the Humanities.

too heavy for the maker to lift." That simple, homely, everyday predicate raises the question: Can God make something too heavy for the maker to lift? The difficulty for the concept of omnipotence that is raised by this question lies in the paradox generated from answering it. Cowan's version of the paradox is:

(A) (i) If God cannot make something too heavy for the maker to lift, then God is not omnipotent since there is something (namely this) which He cannot do.

(ii) If God can make something too heavy for the maker to lift, then God is not omnipotent since there is something else (namely lift everything) which He cannot do.

(iii) So in any case God cannot be omnipotent.

This paradox shows that God cannot be omnipotent because there is a simple, straightforward, non-self-contradictory predicate which describes a task that God cannot perform. Nor will it do, Cowan claims, to rely on the argument against this paradox presented by Bernard Mayo[3] and George Mavrodes.[4] Their argument shows that the statement that God is both omnipotent and able to make something He cannot lift is self-contradictory and, hence, that the paradox of omnipotence contains a self-contradiction. According to Cowan it will not do to rely on this argument because Mayo and Mavrodes are quite correct in holding that the paradox contains a self-contradiction. Nevertheless, the paradox still constitutes a valid objection to the doctrine of omnipotence because it is demonstrable that the concept of omnipotence is itself self-contradictory and this accounts for the fact that the paradox contains a contradiction. So Cowan's strategy to sustain the paradox of omnipotence is to argue that it is self-contradictory to claim that God can do anything the description of which is not self-contradictory.

His argument rests on presenting two formal deductions that appear to be unquestionably valid. The first deduction has two premises. The first premise is one which Cowan claims is true by definition and it is a principle which Cowan refers to as (1). That principle, (1), states that there are perfectly respectable, non-self-contradictory predicates which are such that the capacity of an individual to have them truly predicated of himself logically excludes the capacity to have other similarly non-self-contradictory predicates truly predicated of himself. Cowan states the principle formally as: $(\exists F)\ (\exists G)\ (x)\ (pFx \supset \sim pGx)$ where 'pFx' means 'x' can (do or be) 'F' and where the range of the variables 'F' and 'G' is limited to the non-self-contradictory.

One example of the sort of thing referred to in (1) is the manufacturing ability we have been considering. If one can make something one cannot lift, one cannot lift everything (collectively or distributively) that one can make. It is important to note, moreover, that the existence of such mutually exclusive predicates is a matter of logic. If we did not have them already, we could define some. Thus (1) is not merely true, it is a logical truth in the sense of being true by (following logically from) definitions.[5]

The second premise is the assumption that God is omnipotent, that God can do anything the description of which is not self-contradictory. From these two premises Cowan validly deduces, by the rules of logic alone, that there is at least one thing that God both can do and cannot do. He instantiates this conclusion by saying the following:

> For example, since God is omnipotent and thus can make any kind of thing, He can make something He cannot lift; but since He is omnipotent and thus can lift any kind of thing, He cannot make something He cannot lift.[6]

The second deduction has just one premise, principle (1) from the first deduction true by definition, and does not rely on the assumption that God is omnipotent. This deduction is intended to show that Mavrodes is wrong in his claim that the paradox of omnipotence *must* begin either with the assumption that God is not omnipotent or with the assumption that God is omnipotent. From this principle true by definition Cowan validly deduces, by the rules of logic alone, that for *every* individual there will be *something* or other that the individual cannot do. He instantiates this conclusion by saying the following: "Since no one can make something he cannot lift unless he cannot lift everything, everyone (including God) will be limited either with respect to his making or with respect to his lifting or both.[7]

Cowan reasons that since (1) is a logical truth and since the first deduction follows from (1) and the assumption that God is omnipotent by the rules of logic alone, the first deduction shows that it is self-contradictory to assume that God (or anything else) is omnipotent. Furthermore, since (1) is a logical truth and since the second deduction shows that from (1) it follows by the rules of logic alone that nothing is omnipotent, it is a logical truth that nothing is omnipotent and, hence, the claim that God is omnipotent is self-contradictory. Accordingly, the concept of omnipotence is itself self-contradictory and so the paradox of omnipotence does indeed constitute a valid objection to the doctrine of omnipotence.

Given this general strategy Cowan presumably thinks that there are predicates which are not self-contradictory and which, even though they are not self-contradictory, yet raise difficulties for the concept of omniscience, the concept which entails that God knows everything. It would appear that he regards the predicate 'knowing how to create a universe the potentialities of which the creator does not know' as one such predicate and that the predicate raises the question: Does God know how to create a universe the potentialities of which He does not know? Presumably the difficulty for the concept of omniscience that is raised by this question lies in a paradox generated from answering it, a paradox which, one would suppose, would parallel the one contained in argument (A) above for the concept of omnipotence. That is, an answer to this question would appear to generate the following argument:

(B) (i) If God does not know how to create a universe the poten-
          tialities of which He does not know, then God is not omniscient
          since there is something (namely this) which He does not
          know.
     (ii) If God does know how to create a universe the potential-
          ities of which He does not know, then God is not omniscient
          since there is something else (namely the potentialities of the
          universe in question) which He does not know.
    (iii) So in any case God cannot be omniscient.

So given Cowan's general strategy with respect to the concept of omnipotence and his few remarks quoted above about the concept of omniscience, it would appear that argument (B), or something very much like it, constitutes what Cowan would acknowledge to be the paradox of omniscience. Furthermore, it would appear that Cowan thinks that this paradox shows that God cannot be omniscient because there is a simple, straightforward, non-self-contradictory predicate which describes something that God cannot know. Presumably either God cannot know the potentialities of every possible universe or God cannot know how to create a universe the potentialities of which He does not know and, Cowan seems to think, both of these entail that God is not omniscient.

But if argument (B) is the argument Cowan has in mind when he suggests that there is a paradox of omniscience, then it is not at all clear that his suggestion is correct because it is not at all clear that (i) and

(ii) of argument (B) are true. Since the claim that God knows how to create a universe the potentialities of which He does not know does actually entail the claim that God cannot know the potentialities of every possible universe, (ii) is true if and only if the latter claim further entails that God is not omniscient and (ii) [is] false if that latter claim does *not entail* that God is not omniscient. In other words, premise (ii) of argument (B) is true if and only if it is true that

(a) *x* is omniscient

entails

(b) *x* knows the potentialities of every possible universe.

Since knowing the potentialities of a possible universe entails and is entailed by knowing the truth-values (that is, true or false) of every future contingent proposition about that possible universe, (b) entails and is entailed by

(c) for every future contingent proposition *P* about any possible universe, *x* knows that *P* is true or *x* knows that *P* is false.

So (ii) of argument (B) is true if and only if it is true that (a) entails (c). However, it would appear that (a) does not entail (c).

I assume that the concept of omniscience is to be explained in something like the following way:

(K) *x* is omniscient if and only if for every proposition *P*, if *P* is true then *x* knows that *P* is true, if *P* is false then *x* knows that *P* is false, and if *P* is neither true nor false then *x* knows that *P* is neither true nor false.

Now if (K) is correct and it is true that

(d) future contingent propositions are neither true nor false,

then for any omniscient being *x* it is true that

(e) for every future contingent proposition *P* about any possible universe, *x* knows that *P* is neither true nor false

because (a), (K), and (d) jointly entail (e). Notice that (e) entails that *x* does not know the potentialities of *any* possible universe, so the claim that *x* does not know the potentialities of every possible universe is not only consistent with the omniscience of *x* but is actually entailed by the omniscience of *x* if (d) is true. Since (c) and (e) cannot both be true for any given instantiation of x and since (e) is true if (a), (K), and (d) are true, it follows for any given instantiation of x that it is possible for (a) to be true and (c) false and, hence, that it is possible for (a) to be true and (b) false. It is possible for God to be omniscient and not know the potentialities of *any* possible universe.

In fact if (d) is true then neither God nor anyone else can know the potentialities of any possible universe because the future is logically unknowable if (d) is true. Assume that (d) is actually true, that future contingent propositions are neither true nor false, then the future is logically unknowable because knowing something about the future would entail either knowing that some proposition about the future is true or knowing that it is false and this would entail that some future contingent proposition is either true or false. But then by assumption some future contingent proposition would be *both* neither true nor false *and* either true or false. It follows from this that if (d) is true, then it is logically impossible to know the future and also that it is logically impossible for anyone to know the potentialities of any possible universe. If (d) is true, then the claim that God does not know the potentialities of every possible universe does not count against or falsify the claim that He is omniscient. The claim that God does not know the potentialities of every possible universe can count against or falsify the claim that He is omniscient only if it is possible to know the potentialities of a possible universe and the latter is possible only if (d) is false. Consequently, since it is possible for (a) to be true and (b) false, (a) does not entail (b) and so (ii) is false and argument (B) does not show that God cannot be omniscient. Argument (B), then, does not constitute a paradox of omniscience. If argument (B) is the argument Cowan has in mind when he suggests that there is a paradox of omniscience, then his suggestion is misguided.

However, it might be that Cowan has a different argument in mind. Notice that because (a), (K), and the negation of (d) do jointly entail (c) and (b), the argument (B1) results if we take (i) and (iii) from (B) and substitute for premise (ii) in (B) the premise (ii′):

> (ii′) If God does know how to create a universe the potentialities of which He does not know *and* future contingent propositions are either true or false, then God is not omniscient since there is something (namely the truth-values of the future contingent propositions about the universe in question) which He does not know.

Perhaps (B1) is the argument Cowan has in mind when he suggests that there is a paradox of omniscience. If (B1) is his argument then he will have established that God cannot be omniscient and that there is a paradox of omniscience only if (i) is true and (d) is false, for (ii′) is true *only if* (d) is false. But is (d) false? There is no easy answer to this question because if (d) is false, it is not at all obvious that it is false and so it is not at all clear that (ii′) of (B1) is true. Indeed, while some philosophers have argued that (d) is false, others have argued that it is true[8] and, as far as I know, no one has yet provided a conclusive solution to the problem, so there is no conclusive reason to judge that (d) is false. Thus there is no apparent reason for accepting the negation of (d) and the negation of (d) is essential to the claim that (B1) constitutes a paradox of omniscience. In order to conclusively sustain (B1) it would be necessary for the proponent of (B1) to come up with a decisive proof which shows that future contingent propositions are either true or false. Exactly what such a proof would look like is not at all clear, but without such a proof the proponent of argument (B1) cannot justifiably claim to have come up with a paradox of omniscience because without such a proof no one is compelled to accept (ii′) and no one is compelled to accept the conclusion of (B1). So, if (B1) is the argument Cowan has in mind when he suggests that there is a paradox of omniscience, then he needs a proof for the claim that future contingent propositions are either true or false in order to sustain his view that there is a paradox of omniscience.

Let us assume for the sake of argument, that Cowan has just such a proof, that is, that he can conclusively establish that (d) is false. Assume that the proof is so decisive that anyone would have to be defiant of reason itself to subscribe to (d). Even under these optimum conditions for the negation of (d), (B1) will constitute a paradox of omniscience if and only if (i) is true and it is not clear yet that (i) *is* true. For (i) is true if and only if the claim that God does not know how to create a universe the potentialities of which He does not know does in fact entail that God is not omniscient and (i) is false if that claim *does not entail* that God is not omniscient. In other words premise (i) of argument (B1) is true if and only if it is true that (a) (*x* is omniscient) entails

(f) *x* knows how to create a universe the potentialities of which God does not know.

We have already seen that (a) does not entail (b) and it would appear that (a) does not entail (f) either. For if it is true that

(g) there is no way to create a universe the potentialities of which God does not know

then for any omniscient being x it is true that

(h) x knows that there is no way to create a universe the potentialities of which God does not know

because (a), (K), and (g) jointly entail (h). Notice that (h) entails that x does not know how to create a universe the potentialities of which God does not know, so the claim that x does not know how to create such a universe is not only consistent with the omniscience of x but is actually entailed by the omniscience of x if (g) is true. Since (f) and (h) cannot both be true for any given instantiation of x and since (h) is true if (a), (K), and (g) are true, it follows for any given instantiation of x that it is possible for (a) to be true and (f) false. It is possible for God to be omniscient and not know how to create a universe the potentialities of which He does not know.

In fact if (g) is true then neither God nor anyone else can know how to create such a universe because how to create such a universe is logically unknowable if (g) is true. Assume that (g) is actually true, that there is no way to create a universe the potentialities of which God does not know, then how to create such a universe is logically unknowable because knowing how to create such a universe would entail knowing that there is a way to create such a universe and this would entail that (g) is false. Then by assumption, (g) would be *both* true *and* false. It follows from this that if (g) is true, then it is logically impossible to know how to create a universe the potentialities of which God does not know. If (g) is true then the claim that God does not know how to create such a universe does not count against or falsify the claim that He is omniscient. The claim that God does not know how to create such a universe can count against or falsify the claim that He is omniscient only if it is possible to know how to create such a universe and the latter is possible only if (g) is false. Consequently, since it is possible for (a) to be true and (f) false, (a) does not entail (f) and so (i) is false and argument (B1) does not establish that God cannot be omniscient. Argument (B1), then, does not constitute a paradox of omniscience. If argument (B1) is the argument Cowan has in mind when he suggests that there is a paradox of omniscience, then we are once again forced to the conclusion that his suggestion is misguided.

Perhaps Cowan has yet a different argument in mind. Since (a), (K), and the denial of (g) do jointly entail (f), the argument (B2) results if we take (ii′) and (iii) from (B1) and substitute for premise (i) in (B1) the premise (i′):

(i′) If God does not know how to create a universe the potentialities of which He does not know *and* there is a way to create such a universe, then God is not omniscient since there is something (namely how to create such a universe) which He does not know.

It may be that (B2) is the argument Cowan has in mind when he suggests that there is a paradox of omniscience. If (B2) is his argument then he will have established that God cannot be omniscient and that there is a paradox of omniscience *only if* (g) is false, for (i′) is true only if (g) is false.

But there does not appear to be any reason for thinking that (g) is false. It would not appear to entail a contradiction or to be counterintuitive to hold that (g) is true. There are no obvious philosophical or theological truths with which (g) would appear to be logically incompatible. Moreover, it seems quite plain that empirical evidence is not even relevant to deciding the truth-value of (g). One might argue that (g) is false on the grounds that the denial of (g) is logically possible and whatever is logically possible is also causally possible. This latter principle, however, would seem to be at least as problematic as the denial of (g) itself and would seem to constitute a rather slender thread upon which to hang the claim that God cannot be omniscient. As a matter of fact it is not entirely unexceptionable to hold that the denial of (g) is logically possible. In any case the principle that whatever is logically possible is also causally possible is exceptionable enough so that the traditional theist need not feel any qualms at all in dismissing it as an inadequate reason for rejecting the doctrine of divine omniscience. Thus it is quite plausible to subscribe to (g) and (g) may very well be true.

In fact it is quite easy to think of conditions logically compatible with the central claims of traditional theism that might obtain and that entail that (g) *is true*. Assume that *at the present moment* God has the property of being omniprescient[9] where the property of being omniprescient is the property a being has just in case that being is omniscient with respect to everything knowable about the future. If the future is in principle entirely unknowable, then it follows that every being capable of cognition is vacuously omniprescient since such a being would vacuously know everything knowable about the future. Furthermore the fact that a being is omniprescient at the present moment is compatible with the fact that there is some true proposition about the past or present which the omniprescient being does not know to be true, so the assumption that at the present moment God has the property of being omniprescient does not entail either that God is omniscient or that God is not omniscient.

Now if (d) is false and God is omniprescient at the present moment, then it would appear that (g) is true. For if future contingent propositions are either true or false and God is omniprescient at the present moment, then God knows the truth-values of *all* future contingent propositions about *every* possible universe. It follows from this that there is *no* possible universe whose future contingent propositions are such that God does not know their truth-values and this entails that there is no way to create a universe the potentialities of which God does not know. The result is that if (d) is false and God is omniprescient at the present moment, then (g) is true and (i') of (B2) is false becaue (i') entails that (g) is false.

Yet there is a really more serious difficulty with (B2) on our assumption. Recall that (ii') requires that (d) be false by virtue of the fact that the antecedent of (ii') asserts the denial of (d), that is, it asserts that future contingent propositions are either true or false. Now since the denial of (d) and the claim that God is omniprescient at the present moment jointly entail (g) and since (i') entails the denial of (g), it follows that (i') and (ii') jointly entail both (g) and the denial of (g) on our assumption. If it is true that God is omniprescient at the present moment then, even if we do not assume that God is omniscient, argument (B2) contains a contradiction and does not establish that God *cannot* be omniscient. In addition, since the denial of (d) and the claim that God is omniscient jointly entail that God is omniprescient, exactly the same consequences follow if God is omniscient. In order to escape these consequences and to sustain the claim that (B2) constitutes a paradox of omniscience, it would be necessary for the proponent of (B2) to argue that (B2) contains a contradiction by virtue of the fact that the concept of omniscience is itself self-contradictory.

If Cowan's argument for the paradox of omnipotence is actually applicable to (B2), then this is the move that he must have in mind for showing that (B2) is a paradox of omniscience and that the paradox does in fact constitute a valid objection to the doctrine of divine omniscience. If Cowan is correct then it is to be supposed that the concept of omniscience is *demonstrably* self-contradictory and that this accounts for the fact that (B2) contains a contradiction. It is apparently to be supposed that there are two formal and valid deductions which show that it is self-contradictory to claim that God knows everything knowable. The first deduction would have two premises. The first premise, (1'), would be one that is true by definition and the second premise would be the assumption that God is omniscient, that God knows everything knowable. From these premises it would be validly deducible, by the rules of logic alone, that there is at least one thing that God both knows and cannot know. The second deduction would have just one premise, (1'), the first premise from the first deduction that is true by definition, and would not rely on the assumption that God is omniscient. This deduction would presumably overcome or forestall any claim to the effect that a paradox of omniscience *must* begin either with the assumption that God is not omniscient or with the assumption that God is omniscient. From premise (1') which is true by definition it would be validly deducible, by the rules of logic alone, that for *every* individual there will be *something* or other that the individual cannot know.

Presumably premise (1') that is common to both of these deductions and true by definition will be *logically true* in the sense that it is true by virtue of the fact that it follows logically from definitions. Since (1') will be a logical truth and since the first deduction will follow by the rules of logic alone from (1') and the assumption that God is omniscient, the first deduction will show that it is self-contradictory to assume that God (or anything else) is omniscient. Also since (1') will be a logical truth and the second deduction will show that from (1') it follows by the rules of logic alone that nothing is omniscient, the second deduction will show that it is a *logical truth* that nothing is omniscient and thus it will show that the claim that God is omniscient is self-contradictory. It is to be supposed that in this way it can be shown that the concept of omniscience is self-contradictory and that there is a paradox of omniscience which does indeed constitute a valid objection to the doctrine of divine omniscience. Presumably Cowan thinks that there is a principle, (1'), that corresponds to (1) by virtue of its logical properties and that it is related to argument (B2) as (1) is related to the paradox of omnipotence. In other words it would seem that Cowan thinks that there is a logically true principle about knowledge which entails, and from which it can be deduced by the rules of logic alone, that it is self-contradictory either to assume or to claim that God is omniscient. It would appear that in order to assess Cowan's claims that there is a paradox of omniscience and that his argument about the paradox of omnipotence is applicable to it, we need to know whether or not there is any such principle as (1′) and, if there is, what it is like.

Recall that Cowan's principle (1) for the paradox of omnipotence states that there are some capacities that logically imply limitations, that there are some things one can do only if one cannot do certain other things, or, more formally, $(\exists F)\,(\exists G)\,(x)\,(pFx \supset \sim pGx)$ ('pFx' means 'x can do or be F'). Cowan thinks that this principle is logically true and that its individual variable can be instantiated with respect to persons and that its predicate variables can be instantiated with respect to a person's lifting and manufacturing capacities. For instance, he thinks that "if God can make something He cannot lift then God cannot lift everything He can make" and "if God can lift everything then God cannot make something He cannot lift" are both substitution instances of (1) and that they both entail that there is a performable act that God cannot perform. Now if one were to regard knowing as a kind of capacity and a kind of doing, then principle (1) could be read as a principle about knowledge. Perhaps Cowan is to be taken quite literally when he claims that his argument about omnipotence is applicable to omniscience. Perhaps he means that principle (1) and his two deductions are applicable to the concept of omniscience by virtue of the fact that the individual variable can be instantiated with respect to persons and the predicate variables can be instantiated with respect to a person's knowing capacities. It may be that (1′) is to be taken as a special case of (1) so that when (1) is applied to the concept of omniscience we are to read the word 'know' for the word 'do' in (1). Presumably (1′) is to be regarded as a version of (1) where (1′) states that there are some things one can *know* only if one cannot *know* certain other things and where 'pFx' of the more formal statement now means 'x can *know* F.' If this is a correct understanding of Cowan's claim concerning the applicability of his argument to the concept of omniscience, then it would appear that he thinks that his two deductions establish that the concept of omniscience is self-contradictory if we instantiate the predicate variables with respect to knowing.

In order to assess this claim let us inspect Cowan's two deductions. His first deduction goes as follows:

(1)	$(\exists F)\,(\exists G)\,(x)\,(pFx \supset \sim pGx)$	By definition.
(2)	$(F)pFg$	Assumption that God is omnipotent. 'F' again restricted to the non-self-contradictory.
(3)	$pFg \supset \sim pGg$	From (1) by instantiation.

(4) pFg	From (2) by instantiation.
(5) ~pGg	From (3) and (4) by *modus ponens*.
(6) pGg	From (2) by instantiation.[10]

His second deduction is this:

(1) (∃F)(∃G)(x)(pFx ⊃ ~pGx)	By definition.
(2) pFx ⊃ ~pGx	By existential instantiation on F and G, and universal instantiation on x.
(3) pFx	Conditional proof assumption.
(4) ~pGx	By *modus ponens* from (2) and (3).
(5) (∃F)~pFx	Existential generalization from (4).
(6) pFx ⊃ (∃F)~pFx	Conditional proof from (3)–(5).
(7) ~pFx	Conditional proof assumption.
(8) (∃F)~pFx	Existential generalization from (7).
(9) ~pFx ⊃ (∃F)~pFx	Conditional proof from (7)–(8).
(10) pFx v ~pFx	Tautology.
(11) (∃F)~pFx	By constructive dilemma from (6), (9), and (10).
(12) ~(F)pFx	By quantifier negation from (11).
(13) (x)~(F)pFx	Universal generalization from (12).
(14) ~(∃x)(F)pFx	By quantifier negation from (13).
or (14a) (x)(∃F)~pFx	By quantifier negation from (13).[11]

If Cowan's first deduction does actually apply to the concept of omniscience then line (2) requires some modification. Line (2) must be modified to state that it is the assumption that God is omniscient. But even with this modification of line (2) it would appear to be wrong to claim that the first deduction shows that it is self-contradictory to assume that God is omniscient. It would be wrong to make this claim because the claim relies on the assumption that universal instantiation is, without qualification, valid for line (2) when (2) is taken as the assumption that God is omniscient and it would appear that universal instantiation is not, without qualification, valid under these circumstances. Suppose that we substitute for 'pFx' the sentence 'God can know that David Hume is alive' and for 'pGx' the sentence 'God can know that Plato is alive.' With these substitutions, line (3) is read as the true sentence

(3′) If God can know that David Hume is alive then He cannot know that Plato is alive.

But then lines (4) and (6) cannot be validly deduced from (2) by universal instantiation because the claim that God is omniscient does not entail either

(4′) God can know that David Hume is alive

or

(6′) God can know that Plato is alive.

These entailments do not hold because 'David Hume is alive' and 'Plato is alive' are both false and the concept of omniscience does not entail that an omniscient being can know a proposition to be true that is in fact false. Universal instantiation is not, without qualification, valid for line (2) of the first deduction when (2) is read as the assumption that God is omniscient. It follows that lines (4), (5), and (6) cannot be validly deduced from the preceding lines and this entails that the first deduction does not establish that it is self-contradictory to assume that God is omniscient.

However it may be that the first deduction can be modified still further in order to overcome this difficulty. The claim that a statement, S, is true and the claim that God is omniscient jointly entail that God knows that S is true. So if we add to line (2) the statement that 'F' is restricted to what is true or to what is knowable, then universal instantiation is valid for line (2) of the first deduction when that line is read as the assumption that God is omniscient if we instantiate only with respect to what is true or knowable. Modifying (2) in this way overcomes the above difficulty. But even with that modification the first deduction does not establish that it is self-contradictory, or even that it is false, to assume that God is omniscient unless there is a true instantiation of line (1) whose antecedent is entailed by the claim that God is omniscient and whose consequent entails that there is something knowable that God cannot know. It is clear that the instantiations Cowan has in mind will not do. For both

(j) if God can know how to create a universe the potentialities of which He does not know then God cannot know the potentialities of every possible universe,

and

(k) if God can know the potentialities of every possible universe then God cannot know how to create a universe the potentialities of which He does not know fail to satisfy either of these conditions. As we have already seen, the claim that God is omniscient does not entail either the antecedent of (j) or the antecedent of (k) and the claim that there is something knowable that God cannot know is not entailed by either the consequent of (j) or the consequent of (k). Thus neither (j) nor (k) have an antecedent that would be a valid instantiation of (2) and neither of them have a consequent that entails that God is not omniscient. In short, Cowan's suggested instantiations of (1) will not do and it is not at all obvious that there is any instantiation that will do. In the absence of any true instantiation of line (1) that satisfies the required conditions his first deduction cannot be applied to the concept of omniscience either to establish that it is self-contradictory to assume that God is omniscient or even to establish that it is false that God is omniscient. Having failed to identify an adequate instantiation, Cowan is wrong to claim that his first deduction applies to the concept of omniscience and that the deduction shows that the concept is self-contradictory.

The second deduction suffers a similar difficulty. The problem with the second deduction lies with lines (5) and (8). Line (5) is the existential quantification of an expression which follows from line (2), the instantiation of line (1), and an assumption for conditional proof. Line (8) is the existential quantification of an assumption for conditional proof. Both (5) and (8) assert the same existentially quantified proposition which is carried through to the conclusions of the deduction and there are at least two different ways of reading that proposition. Either that proposition asserts that there is some sentence (something) that x cannot know to be true (that x cannot know) or that proposition asserts that there is some *true* sentence (something *knowable*) that x cannot know to be true (that x cannot know). If (5) and (8) are to be read in the first way then the last two lines of the second deduction do not entail that x is not omniscient because the claim that x does not know some sentence, S, to be true or does not know something, T, does not entail that there is something knowable that x does not know unless S is indeed true or T is indeed knowable. If, for example, lines (4) and (7) are the sentence 'x cannot know that Plato is alive' then lines (5) and (8), the existential quantification of that sentence, assert that there is some proposition ('Plato is alive') that x cannot know to be true and the last line, (14a), asserts that there is a proposition ('Plato is alive') that no one can know to be true. But that assertion, that x cannot know (no one can know) it to be true that Plato is alive, does not entail that x is not (no one is) omniscient because that assertion does not entail that there is something knowable that x does not know (that no one knows). If (5) and (8) are to be read in the first way then the last two lines of the second deduction do not establish that no one can be omniscient unless Cowan can come up with a true instantiation of line (1) whose consequent entails that x cannot know to be true (cannot know) some proposition that is unquestionably true (something that is unquestionably knowable). Again, Cowan's suggested instantiations, (j) and (k), will not do. In the absence of any adequate instantiation of line (1), the second deduction fails to show that the concept of omniscience is self-contradictory on this first reading of lines (5) and (8).

On the other hand, if (5) and (8) are to be read in the second way then existential quantification is valid over the expression 'pFx' when it is read as 'x can *know* F' only if 'F' denotes either sentences that are actually true or something that is actually knowable. Under this reading line (5) will be a valid move in the second deduction only if 'G' in line (4) denotes what is actually true or knowable and 'G' will denote this only if line (4) follows from a true instantiation of line (1) whose consequent entails that x cannot know to be true (cannot know) some proposition that is actually true (something that is actually knowable). Consequently, if (5) and (8) are read in the second way, it follows that the last two lines of the second deduction do not establish that no one can be omniscient unless Cowan can come up with a true instantiation of (1) that satisfies the required conditions. In the absence of any adequate instantiation of line (1), Cowan's second deduction fails to show that the concept of omniscience is self-contradictory even on this second reading of lines (5) and (8) and it is most unlikely that there are any other readings of (5) and (8) that would escape this difficulty and yet entail that there is something knowable that x does not know.

It turns out that Cowan's two deductions do not apply to the concept of omniscience. In the absence of any true instantiation of line (1) whose antecedent is entailed by the claim that some being x is omniscient and whose consequent entails that there is something knowable that x cannot know, his argument concerning the paradox of omnipotence does not establish either that the concept of omniscience is self-contradictory or that it is self-contradictory to assume or to claim that God is omniscient. In short, Cowan's argument cannot be used to defend the claim that the contradiction in (B2) is due to the fact that the concept of omniscience is itself self-contradictory and so his argument cannot be used to sustain the claim that (B2) constitutes a paradox of omniscience. If (B2) is the argument Cowan has in mind when he suggests that there is a paradox of omniscience, then his suggestion is wrong. Arguments (B), (B1), and (B2) all fail to constitute a paradox of omniscience and in the absence of any other alternatives he is wrong to claim that there is a paradox of omniscience.

The final result is twofold. First, since there does not appear to be any reason for thinking that there is a true instantiation of (1) that satisfies the required conditions, there does not appear to be any reason for thinking that Cowan's argument concerning the paradox of omnipotence does apply to the concept of omniscience and so his claim that it does apply must be rejected. Second, since there does not appear to be any promising alternative to (B), (B1), and (B2), there does not appear to be any reason whatsoever for thinking that there is a paradox of omniscience which constitutes a valid objection to the doctrine of divine omniscience and so his claim that there is such a paradox must be rejected.

NOTES

1. J. L. Cowan, "The Paradox of Omnipotence," *Analysis* 25 (Supp.), no. 3 (January 1965): 102–108.
2. Cowan, p. 108.
3. Bernard Mayo, "Mr. Keene on Omnipotence," *Mind* 70, no. 278 (April 1961): 249–50.
4. George Mavrodes, "Some Puzzles Concerning Omnipotence," *Philosophical Review* 72, no. 2 (April 1963): 221–23.
5. Cowan, p. 104.
6. Cowan, p. 105.
7. Cowan, p. 106.
8. For numerous discussions of the problem of future contingents see the extensive bibliographies in Richard M. Gale, ed., *The Philosophy of Time* (London: Macmillan, 1968), pp. 506–11, and Steven M. Cahn, *Fate, Logic, and Time* (New Haven: Yale University Press, 1967), pp. 139–45. For further references consult the subject heading "Future" in *The Philosopher's Index.*
9. For a more complete discussion of what I call the doctrine of divine omniprescience see my "Omniprescience and Divine Determinism," *Religious Studies* 12, no. 3. (September 1976): 365–81, and my "Divine Omniprescience: Are Literary Works Eternal Entities?" *Religious Studies* 15 (1979): 281–87.
10. Cowan, p. 105.
11. Cowan, pp. 105–106.

14

Wainwright, Augustine, and God's Simplicity: A Final Word

Professor Wainwright presents three objections[1] to my account[2] of Augustine's attempt to explicate the doctrine that God is simple. I shall answer these objections in the order that they are presented.

His first objection is that I have not shown that a contradiction is entailed by what appears to be Augustine's attempt to formulate a distinction between relative and non-relative properties. Wainwright formally reconstructs my argument against what I take to be the two possible ways suggested by Augustine for formulating that distinction and then points out a difficulty with my argument. The difficulty is that premise (5), *The entity worshipped by Augustine is God,* and premise (12), *The property I am thinking of is omniscience,* are true, but only contingently true. What follows from this is that premises (1) and (2), the two formulations of the distinction in question, have not been shown to be *self*-contradictory because it has not been shown that (1) by itself or (2) by itself (along with necessary truths and the laws of logic) entails a contradiction. All my argument establishes is that (1) and (5) jointly entail the contradiction in line (9) and that (2) and (12) jointly entail the contradiction in line (16). In short, Wainwright's point is that in order to show that (1) and (2) are logically incoherent I must show that they are self-contradictory and to do this I must show that a contradiction is deducible from each of those premises by appealing only to them and to necessary truths and

From *The New Scholasticism* 53, no. 1 (Winter 1979): 124–27. Reprinted by permission.

the laws of logic. Wainwright is quite correct on this point and I am grateful to him for exposing this defect in my argument.

However, this defect is not as serious as it may first appear to be because it is easily enough corrected by considering slightly different counter-examples. Rather than considering *the entity worshipped by Augustine* consider instead *the entity worshipped by Augustine when Augustine worships God;* and rather than considering *the property I am thinking of* consider instead *the property I am thinking of when I am thinking of omniscience.* With these changes Wainwright's formal reconstruction of my argument can be restated by simply replacing premises (3), (4), (5), (10), (11), and (12) with the following re-statements of them:

(3′) 'The entity worshipped by Augustine when Augustine worships God is omniscient' is a statement that refers to a being not identical to the entity worshipped by Augustine when Augustine worships God, *viz.,* Augustine.

(4′) *Omniscience* is relative with respect to the entity worshipped by Augustine when Augustine worships God. (From 1 and 3′.)

(5′) The entity worshipped by Augustine when Augustine worships God is God.

(10′) 'God has the property I am thinking of when I am thinking of omniscience' is a statement containing a predicate that refers to a being not identical to God, *viz.,* William Wainwright.

(11′) *The property I am thinking of when I am thinking of omniscience* is relative with respect to God. (From 2 and 10′.)

(12′) The property I am thinking of when I am thinking of omniscience is omniscience.

When these reformulated premises are substituted for their counterparts in Wainwright's reconstruction of my argument, line (6) follows from (4′) and (5′), line (13) follows from (11′) and (12′), and the deductions from lines (6) through (9) and from lines (13) through (16) follow as they did before the substitutions. These revisions correct the defect in the original formulation of my argument because the contradictions derived in lines (9) and (16) now follow from (1) and (2) respectively by appealing to *only* necessary truths and the laws of logic since (5′) and (12′) are necessary truths. So, it turns out that I am correct in claiming that (1) and (2) are logically incoherent and cannot be true.

Wainwright's second objection is that (1) and (2) do not provide the only plausible formulations of the distinction between relative and nonrelative properties. In rebuttal he proposes (2′), a revision of my original (2), as a satisfactory formulation of that distinction. I am not altogether clear just how it is that (2′) is supposed to overcome the difficulties raised by my argument as it was originally stated, but my lack of understanding on this point is not important at this juncture because it seems quite clear that (2′) will not do, given the revisions in my argument that were just made above. Formulation (2′) will not do because *omniscience* is necessarily identical with *the property I am thinking of when I am thinking of omniscience* and the statement 'God has the property I am thinking of when I am thinking of omniscience' is a statement the predicate of which refers to a being not identical to God, *viz.,* La Croix. So, by the second disjunct of (2′), *omniscience* is a relative property with respect to God. But Augustine wants to maintain that omniscience is non-relative with respect to God and so he cannot subscribe to Wainwright's (2′). It turns out that Wainwright has not provided a suitable formulation of the distinction between relative and non-relative properties.

The third and final objection presented by Wainwright is that there is a different interpretation of Augustine's account of the doctrine of God's simplicity that is preferable to my own interpretation. According to Wainwright I explicate Augustine's doctrine of God's simplicity in terms of the doctrine that God possesses His non-relative properties non-contingently and, Wainwright claims, "while Augustine does indeed believe that these doctrines are *equivalent* (my italics), what he *means* (his italics) by God's simplicity is that God is what He has." But this account of the matter is extremely misleading because it claims a difference where none actually exists. I do not simply explicate Augustine's account of the doctrine of God's simplicity in terms of the doctrine that God possesses His non-relative properties non-contingently. What I explicate in those terms is a specific account of the doctrine that God is simple, namely, Augustine's claim that "a nature is said to be simple on the grounds that it cannot lose any of the properties that it possesses; that is, there is no distinction to be made between what that nature is and the properties that it has" (my translation). (The translation that Wainwright relies on renders this same passage as: "When a nature is called simple we mean that it can have nothing that it can lose; that it cannot be different from what it has.") To be sure I focus on the first part of this claim rather than the second part in an attempt to gain some understanding of Augustine's version of the doctrine that God is simple. I do this by using the distinctions between relative and non-relative properties and contingent and non-contingent properties to explicate the troublesome concept of a nature that cannot lose any of the properties that it possesses. But the passage from Augustine that is quoted above makes it quite clear that he regards the claim "God is simple means (because) He cannot lose any of the properties He possesses" and the claim "God is simple means (because) there is no difference between what He is and what He has" as equivalent claims, whether that equivalence is regarded as logical equivalence or equivalence in meaning. What this shows is that there is no reason at all for thinking, as Wainwright does, that the latter claim asserts what Augustine "means" by saying that God is simple while the former does not. Both of these claims represent what Augustine means by saying that God is simple, for on his view they both mean the same thing. To explicate one is to explicate the other and following the indications provided by Augustine I explicate them in terms of the relative—non-relative and contingent—non-contingent distinctions.

Furthermore, when Wainwright describes his interpretation he says that Augustine's claim that God is simple is to be understood as meaning that God is what He has *non-relatively*. But, since Augustine does not hold that God is identical with His contingent properties, Wainwright must add to the description of his interpretation by saying that Augustine's claim that God is simple means that God is what He has non-relatively *and* non-contingently. In short, Wainwright would appear to be forced into holding that Augustine's doctrine that God is simple is to be understood as meaning that God is what He has, and that "God is what He has" is to be explicated in terms of the distinctions between relative and non-relative properties and contingent and non-contingent properties. So, since on Augustine's view "God is what He has" means the same as "God cannot lose any of the properties that He possesses," there is no reason to think that Wainwright's interpretation is any different from mine let alone preferable.

NOTES

1. "Augustine on God's Simplicity: A Reply to Richard La Croix," *The New Scholasticism* 53, no. 1 (Winter 1979): 118–23.

2. "Augustine on the Simplicity of God," *The New Scholasticism* 51, no. 4 (Autumn 1977): 453–69.

15

Divine Omniprescience:
Are Literary Works Eternal Entities?

There are two quite common views which appear to be embraced by a large number of aestheticians as well as a large number of nonaestheticians. It is quite commonly believed by many of both groups that God is omniscient with respect to the future, that is, that God knows *everything* that will ever occur. I refer to this belief as the doctrine of divine omniprescience.[1] It is also quite common to many of both groups to believe that literary authorship is creative in the sense that by means of his composing activity an author is an agent who brings about the existence of some thing (e.g., a play, a poem, a novel, etc.) which did not exist prior to the composing activity of that agent and which would not exist without the composing activity of that agent or some similar agent. I shall call this belief the doctrine of literary creativity. What does not appear to be recognized is that these two doctrines cannot both be consistently endorsed. I argue that the two doctrines jointly entail a contradiction and I will point out some of the logical consequences of trying to avoid that contradiction.

It seems quite unexceptionable to say that there exists a whole host of compositions. By a composition I mean such a thing as a play, a poem, a novel, an essay, a story, a review, and the like. Despite the difference in kind, it is no more accurate to say that the moon exists than it is

From *Religious Studies* 15 (1979): 28–87. Reprinted by permission of Cambridge University Press. This paper was written under a Faculty Research Fellowship for 1976 from the Research Foundation of the State University of New York.

to say that Shakespeare's play, *Hamlet,* exists. While compositions are nowadays typically written or recorded in some other way, it is not a necessary condition for the existence of a composition that it be written down or recorded. Prior to printing and the practice of maintaining written records, there was an oral tradition for passing on and maintaining compositions such as tales, songs, poems, and the like. It is no less accurate to say that prehistorical compositions once existed than it is to say that historical compositions now exist or once existed. The existence of a written or otherwise recorded copy of a composition is one sufficient condition for the existence of that composition, but it is not a necessary condition for its existence nor is it the only sufficient condition. Other conditions are necessary and, it would seem, sufficient to truly say of a composition that it exists.

It seems quite true to say that a composition exists, whether or not it is in some way recorded, if it is possible for someone to recite all the lines, to provide an aesthetic critique, to provide a grammatical critique, to repunctuate the composition or substitute one word for another in the composition, to describe the content of the composition (e.g., state its story line or theme; name and describe people, places, or things mentioned in it; and so on), to enumerate in their proper order every word and symbol that occurs in the composition and, in the case of compositions like plays, to stage the composition. If these things and others like them can be done then it seems quite clear that the composition in question exists. If I now compose a play or story in my mind, whether or not I record it and whether or not someone else knows that I have composed it, the things and others like them mentioned above can be done and the composition can be truly said to exist. But if the possibility of doing these or other like things for a given composition entails that the composition exists, then the doctrine of divine omniprescience and the doctrine of literary creativity cannot both be true for it is demonstrable that they jointly entail a contradiction. This can be shown by a *reductio ad absurdum* argument.

Consider, as an example of a composition, the play, *Hamlet.* Assume first that William Shakespeare brought about the existence of that play by means of a certain sequence of his composing activities, that the play did not exist prior to his composing activity, and that the play would not exist without his composing activity or the composing activity of Marlowe or Bacon or some other person. Assume second that God is omniprescient. By the second assumption God knew before the creation of the universe such things as that he would create the universe, that in

A.D. 1564 William Shakespeare would be born at Stratford upon Avon, that Shakespeare would marry Anne Hathaway, and so on. Included among the countless numbers of things that God knew before the creation of the universe, by the first assumption, was that in A.D. 1600 Shakespeare would bring about the existence of a play which had no prior existence and that it would be called *Hamlet*. In addition, God knew what the first word of the play would be and that it would be first, what the second word of the play would be and that it would be second, and what each succeeding word or symbol of the play would be and its proper sequential order; and God knew all this before the creation of the universe. So, before the creation of the universe it was possible for God to recite all the lines of *Hamlet*, to provide an aesthetic critique of *Hamlet*, to provide a grammatical critique of *Hamlet*, and so on. It was even possible before the creation of the universe for God to stage the play with his angels (he could have prompted them in their lines) or, in the absence of angels, he could have created some beings for the express purpose of producing *Hamlet*. In short, since the possibility for someone to do the sort of things enumerated above for some given composition entails that the composition exists, then the given assumptions jointly entail that *Hamlet* existed before the creation of the universe and, hence, they also entail that before creation God knew both that *Hamlet* existed and that it existed before the creation of the universe.

But part of the first assumption is that *Hamlet* did not exist prior to A.D. 1600 and so it did not exist prior to the creation of the universe, and it has already been observed that the given assumptions jointly entail that before creation God knew that *Hamlet* did not exist prior to A.D. 1600 and so before creation he knew that it did not exist prior to the creation of the universe. It follows, then, that *Hamlet* both existed and did not exist before creation and that before creation God knew both that *Hamlet* existed before creation and that *Hamlet* did not exist before creation. So, since the two given assumptions jointly entail a contradiction, they cannot both be true; and, since the above *reductio ad absurdum* argument applies to all compositions, it follows that the doctrine of divine omniprescience and the doctrine of literary creativity are logically incompatible.

Given these results it is quite clear that it is impossible to subscribe to both of these doctrines consistently. Either the doctrine of divine omniprescience must be rejected or the doctrine of literary creativity must be rejected. If the former doctrine is rejected in favour of the latter doctrine, then the contradiction is avoided and there does not appear to be any impediment to holding the view that authors bring about the existence of their compositions. However, while rejecting the doctrine of divine omniprescience does not appear to raise any difficulties for the nontheist, it does raise some problems for the orthodox theist, for if that doctrine is false then it follows that God does not know the future. But if the future is indeed knowable, then there is something knowable that God does *not* know and the claim that God is *not* omniprescient entails that God is *not* omniscient. Presumably this result would be entirely unacceptable to the orthodox theist. Consequently, an orthodox theist cannot avoid the contradictory conclusion of the above *reductio ad absurdum* argument by rejecting the doctrine of divine omniprescience *unless* he also endorses the claim that the future is in principle unknowable. With that claim the theist could consistently reject the doctrine of divine omniprescience and subscribe to the doctrine of divine omniscience. He could argue that because the future is in principle unknowable, the claim that God does *not* know the future (that God is *not* omniprescient) does not entail that there is something knowable that God does not know and, hence, it does not entail that God is not omniscient. But, since the claim that the future is in principle unknowable is not at all obviously true and since attempts to prove that claim have not met with unqualified success, this approach to avoiding the contradiction does not appear to be very promising for the theist. Furthermore, orthodox theists traditionally hold that God *does* know the future and so avoiding the contradiction by rejecting the doctrine of divine omniprescience would be entirely unacceptable to most theists. Thus, the theist must either subscribe to the view that the future is in principle unknowable and seek to find solutions to the difficulties of that view, or else reject the doctrine of literary creativity.

If that doctrine is rejected in favour of the doctrine of divine omniprescience, then the contradiction is avoided and the above *reductio ad absurdum* argument does not appear to raise any further obstacles to holding the view that God knows the future. However, there is an important consequence of this way of avoiding the contradiction. Even without assuming the doctrine of literary creativity, the doctrine of divine omniprescience by itself entails that *all* compositions that ever exist(ed) subsequent to creation did also exist prior to creation. For, if a composition existed at any time *after* creation, then *before* creation God already knew everything about the composition that it is necessary to know in order for him to be able to do the sort of things that it is possible to do only if the composition already existed before creation. In other words, if God is omniprescient then no composition will ever exist that did not exist before the creation of the universe. So, a consequence of the view that God knows *everything* about the future is that all compositions existed before creation. What is important about this consequence is what can be said, given that consequence, both about the nature and genesis of compositions and about the relationship that obtains between an author and his composition.

The orthodox theist typically holds not only the doctrine that God is omniprescient but also the doctrine that God is immutable with respect to being omniprescient, that it is impossible for God to be omniprescient at one time and not at another time. From this it follows that God *always* knows everything that will ever occur and so, given the consequence of the doctrine of divine omniprescience that was just noted, it follows for the orthodox theist that all compositions exist for at least exactly the same duration that God exists. In other words, if God is omniprescient and immutable then no composition can fail to exist so long as God exists. Consequently, if a theist avoids the contradiction by adopting the doctrine of divine omniprescience and also holds that God is *immutably omniprescient,* then he is committed to saying that all compositions are at least coeval with God, that all compositions existed before creation and their duration is at least numerically identical with God's duration.

Furthermore, orthodox theists traditionally subscribe to the doctrine that God is eternal, that God has neither a beginning nor an end. Consequently, if a theist avoids the contradiction in question by adopting the doctrine of divine omniprescience and also holds that God is *both* immutably omniprescient *and* eternal, then he is committed to saying that all compositions are coeternal with God, that all compositions existed before creation and always have existed and always will exist.

Given the two possible assumptions that God is immutable and that God is eternal, there are only two possible results of subscribing to the doctrine of divine omniprescience and the consequence which follows from it. If both assumptions are accepted then it follows that compositions are eternal entities and have no beginning. On the other hand, if the assumption that God is immutable is accepted and the assumption that God is eternal is rejected then it follows that compositions *might not* be eternal entities and *might* have a beginning. Similarly, if the assumption that God is eternal is accepted and the assumption that God is immutable is rejected or if both assumptions are rejected then it also follows that compositions might not be eternal entities and might have a beginning. So, if the contradiction in question is avoided by adopting the doctrine of divine omniprescience and its logical consequence that all compositions existed before creation, then only two views are possible about the duration and existence of compositions. It will be necessary to hold either the view that all compositions existed before creation and have no beginning or the view that all compositions existed before creation but have a beginning.

If the former view is the correct one, then it is an obvious consequence of the doctrine of divine omniprescience that an author does not bring about the existence of the compositions which he has written or of which he is the author. For on this view compositions have no beginning and so their existence is not brought about by anything, not even by God. Consequently, a difficulty for any proponent of this view will be the problem of trying to say what is the nature of the relationship that obtains between an author and the eternal entity we call *his* composition. Specifically there will be the problem of trying to say what it is that an author does in relation to a given composition by virtue of which the composition can be properly said to *belong* to him, since a composition cannot, under this view, be said to belong to an author by virtue of the fact that he brings about its existence. There will also be the problem of trying to say why it is that the author of a good composition should be praised and the author of a bad composition should be blamed. Quite clearly the author of a good composition cannot be praised on the grounds that he has brought about the existence of something good and the author of a bad composition blamed on the grounds that he has brought about the existence of something bad. In short, a proponent of this view will have deprived himself of being able to account for the activity of authorship by saying that an author brings about the existence of a composition and so he will bear the burden of having to solve the problems involved in trying to provide some other account of that activity.

On the other hand, if it is correct to say that all compositions existed before creation but have a beginning, then it is an obvious consequence of the doctrine of divine omniprescience that all compositions existed before their authors and the existence of compositions *is* brought about by something. Consequently, the difficulty for any proponent of this view is twofold. There will be the problem of trying to say what is the nature of the relationship that obtains between an author and *his* composition and there will be the problem of trying to say what it is that brings about the existence of compositions. One possible answer satisfies both problems. Perhaps a proponent of this view will want to say that it is the author who brings about the existence of a composition and that an author and his composition stand in the traditionally understood relationship. A proponent of this view might want to say that the argument from divine omniprescience also demonstrates that an effect can precede its cause. He might want to argue that since the doctrine of divine eternity is false and the doctrine of divine omniprescience is true and entails that all compositions existed before creation, then it follows that an effect can precede its cause because it is also true that an author brings about the existence of his compositions. So, it is a possible consequence of the doctrine of divine omniprescience that one can argue for the principle that an effect can precede its cause. But if a proponent of this view eschews that principle, then he too will have deprived himself of being able to account for the activity of authorship by saying that an author brings about the existence of his compositions and so he will bear the same burdens as those borne by the proponents of the former view. He will also bear the further burden of trying to account for the genesis of compositions.

The result is that the doctrine of divine omniprescience and the doctrine of literary creativity are logically incompatible and one or the other of these doctrines must be rejected by both aestheticians and nonaestheticians alike. If the first doctrine is rejected then no problems arise for the nontheist, but the theist, remember, has either the problem of defending the claim that the future is in principle unknowable or the problem of rejecting the traditional belief that God is omniscient. If the second doctrine is rejected then one must endorse and defend either the view that compositions have no beginning and existed before creation or the view that compositions have a beginning even though they existed before creation.

Moreover, the arguments presented here apply *mutatis mutandis* to the doctrine of divine omniscience with exactly the same results. For if God is omniscient then, for every possible language, God knew before creation that the language was possible. Furthermore, before creation he knew every possible word and symbol and every possible combination of words and symbols for every possible language. So, for every composition that would ever exist *after* creation, God knew *before* creation the exact combination of words and symbols that constitutes the composition. It follows, then, that for every composition that would ever exist after creation, God knew before creation everything about the composition that it is necessary to know in order for him to be able to do the sort of things that it is possible to do only if the composition already existed before creation. Thus, if God is omniscient, all compositions existed before the creation of the universe.

NOTE

1. For a discussion of yet other consequences of the doctrine of divine omniprescience see my "Omniprescience and Divine Determinism," *Religious Studies* 12, no. 3 (September 1976): 365–81.

16

Aquinas on God's Omnipresence and Timelessness

The doctrine that God is omnipresent and the doctrine that God is eternal are two doctrines essential to the theology of St. Thomas Aquinas. They are essential to his theology in the sense that Aquinas resolutely maintains that the property of being omnipresent and the property of being eternal are two of the properties which God possesses necessarily, that being omnipresent and being eternal are included in the very essence of God. In other words, to be God is to be, among other things, both omnipresent and eternal. The latter doctrine, that God is eternal, can be understood in at least two different ways. It can be understood either as the claim that God's duration is temporally infinite or as the claim that God is timeless, that God is neither in time nor subject to literal temporal predications. The view that God is timeless is the one supported by St. Thomas and it is also the view most generally accepted by philosophers and theologians in the middle ages, most notably, by Boethius, Augustine, and Anselm.

But if God is indeed omnipresent then it would appear that he must have been in the United Nations Building *yesterday* as well as the day *before* yesterday. And if God was in the United Nations Building *both* yesterday *and* the day before, then it would appear that he is in time and that temporal predications do actually apply to him. So, it would

From *Philosophy and Phenomenological Research* 4, no. 3 (March 1982): 391–99. Reprinted by permission. This paper was written under a Faculty Research Fellowship for 1977 from the Research Foundation of the State University of New York.

appear that God is *not* a timeless being if he is omnipresent and that two doctrines crucial to the theology of Aquinas are logically incompatible.

At this point defenders of Aquinas are almost certain to object to the preceding argument by claiming that the contradiction it establishes is not a real contradiction when the argument is applied to Aquinas and that this apparent contradiction dissolves with a detailed understanding of his explication of the two doctrines in question. I will show that this line of defense does not work. By examining Aquinas' conception of eternity as timelessness and his conception of omnipresence, I will show that the doctrine of divine eternity and the doctrine of divine omnipresence as they are enunciated by Aquinas do indeed jointly entail a contradiction, that the preceding argument actually does apply to St. Thomas.

The most detailed account of eternity provided by Aquinas occurs in the *Summa Theologiae*, part I, question 10. In article 4 of that question he makes it quite clear that on his view eternity is timeless and not simply endless temporal duration by claiming that there are manifest differences between time and eternity. One of the differences consists in the fact that eternity has neither a beginning nor an end while time has both a beginning and an end. But for Aquinas this difference is only an *accidental* difference for he also holds that even though time has both a beginning and an end it might have had no beginning and no end. So, while it is a necessary condition of eternity that it have neither a beginning nor an end that condition is not a sufficient condition of eternity. It is not a sufficient condition because even if it were true that time had no beginning and no end, time and eternity would still not be identical. For Aquinas there would still remain a difference between time and eternity and that difference is for him an *essential* one, not an *accidental* one. The essential difference that obtains between time and eternity is that eternity is *tota simul*,[1] an instantaneous or simultaneous whole, while time is not. So on Aquinas' view eternity is essentially different from time and, hence, on his view eternity is atemporal or timeless and not simply endless temporal duration. Moreover, on this account eternity is essentially different from time and so is timeless by virtue of the fact that it is *tota simul*. But the notion of eternity as *tota simul* is not in itself altogether clear and so the idea that eternity is timeless is not altogether clear. Consequently, understanding St. Thomas's conception of God and eternity as timeless, and understanding the exact nature of the essential difference that is supposed to obtain between time and eternity, requires a clear understanding of his claim that eternity is *tota simul* while time is not.

In article 1 of question 10 Thomas defines time as nothing more than the numbering of motion or change according to before and after; that is, time is nothing but the numbering of successive beginnings and ends in a sequence of changes. Moreover, in both article 1 and article 4 he subscribes to the principle he attributes to Aristotle that time measures only those things beginning and ending in time. In the same passages he also contrasts time and eternity by pointing out that eternity is *tota simul* while, on the other hand, in time there is before and after, that is, there are beginnings and ends. So, it would seem that successiveness is the essential attribute of time for Aquinas; and it would seem that for him time is *not tota simul* by virtue of the fact that there are beginnings and ends (there is successiveness) *in* time while eternity *is tota simul* and, hence, timeless by virtue of the fact that there are no beginnings and ends (there is no successiveness) *in* eternity.

It would appear, then, that there is a second necessary condition of eternity. Not only is it a necessary condition of eternity that eternity *itself* have neither a beginning nor an end, but it is also a necessary condition of eternity that there be no before and after, no beginnings and ends, *in* eternity. Time could, though it in fact does not, satisfy the first of these two necessary conditions of eternity, but time does not and *cannot* satisfy the second one. Time *cannot* satisfy the second one because while the first one marks only an accidental difference between time and eternity, the second one marks *both* the essential difference between time and eternity *and* the essential characteristic of eternity by virtue of which it is *tota simul* or *timeless*. Indeed, it is a sufficient condition of time that it does *not* satisfy the second necessary condition of eternity. That there are beginnings and ends *in* time appears to be the single feature of time which alone distinguishes it essentially from eternity on Aquinas' view; and that there are no beginnings and ends *in* eternity appears to be the single feature of eternity which alone makes it *tota simul* or timeless on his view.[2] Nevertheless, having neither a beginning nor an end *and* being *tota simul* or timeless do *not* jointly entail that a measure is identical to eternity. Even though these two conditions are both necessary conditions of eternity they are not, on the other hand, jointly *sufficient*. For in article 5 of question 10 Aquinas claims that there is yet a third measure which can satisfy *both* of these necessary conditions of eternity, but still differ essentially from *both* eternity *and* time. According to this account the *aevum*, or as I shall call it, demeternity, is a measure which falls midway between time and eternity and both demeternity and the things in it have a beginning, but no end.

However, this feature does not distinguish demeternity as essentially different from either time or eternity because Aquinas holds that having a beginning but no end is only an accidental feature of demeternity, not an essential one, and it marks only an accidental difference both between demeternity and time and between demeternity and eternity. For even if demeternity and the things in it always had existed and always will exist, or even if God should bring demeternity and the things in it to an end, demeternity would still be essentially different from *both* eternity *and* time. It would be essentially different from time and so be timeless, according to Aquinas, by virtue of the fact that demeternity, like eternity, is *tota simul* while time is not *tota simul* (and this would be true even if demeternity had *both* a beginning *and* an end). It would be essentially different from eternity on his view by virtue of the fact that it is possible for demeternity to be connected to or associated with (*conjungi*) before and after or beginnings and ends while before and after or beginnings and ends are not compatible (*neque compatitur*) with eternity; that it, it is not possible for eternity to be in any way connected to or associated with before and after or beginnings and ends. In short, time has beginnings and ends *in* it, demeternity has no beginnings and ends *in* it though it can be connected to or associated with them, and eternity has no beginnings and ends *in* it, neither can it in any way be connected to or associated with them. It turns out, then, that on Thomas's view the necessary *and* jointly sufficient conditions that a measure must satisfy in order to qualify as eternal are that the measure *itself* have neither a beginning nor an end, that there be no beginnings and ends *in* the measure, and that it be impossible for the measure to be in any way connected to or associated with beginnings and ends; and it turns out that on his view the necessary and sufficient condition that a measure must satisfy in order to qualify as *tota simul* or timeless is that there be no beginnings and ends *in* the measure. Moreover, the essential difference between time and eternity turns out to be that time has beginnings and ends *in* it while eternity, being *tota simul* or timeless, does not have beginnings and ends *in* it; the essential difference between time and demeternity turns out to be that time has beginnings and ends *in* it while demeternity, being *tota simul* or timeless, does not have beginnings and ends *in* it but is *only* connected to or associated with beginnings and ends; and the essential difference between eternity and demeternity, both being *tota simul* or timeless, turns out to be that demeternity can be connected to or associated with beginnings and ends while eternity cannot. By comparing them in this manner, then, Aquinas attempts to distinguish his three measures from one another and to characterize the difference between a temporal measure and a timeless measure.

In spite of the confidence with which Aquinas discusses these comparisons, though, it is not at all clear that they actually succeed in making any genuine distinction between the temporal and the timeless. This is unclear because Aquinas never really explains or makes clear what the difference is between actually possessing beginnings and ends (i.e., being temporal) and not possessing them but merely being connected to or associated with beginnings and ends (i.e., being timeless). What he does say about the subject occurs in article 5 of question 10. There he says that demeternity and the things in it have a beginning but *no end* and that time measures those things whose being consists in or is subject to change while demeternity, on the other hand, is the measure of those things whose being neither consists in nor is subject to change *though they are nevertheless connected to or associated with (adjunctam) some actual or potential change.* His examples of demeternal things are the celestial bodies and angels. According to his examples the celestial bodies have unchangeable being though along with this unchangeable being they also *have* changeableness of place. On this same account angels, too, have unchangeable being though along with this unchangeable being they also *have* changeableness of choice at the natural level and changeableness of thoughts, affections, and, in their own mode, place as well. As examples of temporal things Aquinas mentions all movements and even the very being itself of all things capable of having an end (*omnium corruptibilium*).

Presumably, then, Aquinas holds that the things measured by time have changeable being by virtue of the fact that the very being of each of these temporal things has a beginning and an end marking that changeability. According to this understanding time would have beginnings and ends *in* it because the very being itself of everything measured by time has both a beginning *and* an end. Conversely, he holds that the things measured by demeternity have unchangeable being by virtue of the fact that the very being of each of these demeternal things has no beginning *and* end that would mark any changeability in their being. According to this understanding demeternity would have no beginnings and ends *in* it because the very being itself of everything measured by demeternity does not have both a beginning *and* an end though demeternity is connected to or associated with beginnings and ends because the things measured by demeternity have beginnings and ends marked by changes that occur *to* them.

On this account, then, demeternity has no beginnings and ends *in* it and so is *tota simul* by virtue of the fact that the being of demeternal things neither consists in nor is subject to change, that is, has no beginning *and* end. But there are two difficulties with this account of the difference between actually possessing beginnings and ends and not possessing them but merely being connected to or associated with them. First, in article 5 of question 10 Aquinas resolutely maintains that God has it within his power to bring demeternity and the things in it to an end and that having no beginning *and* end is only an *accidental* feature of demeternity and demeternal things. It follows from this that the difference between having no beginnings and ends *in* it and having beginnings and ends *in* it is not an essential difference between demeternity and time. So, that difference does not distinguish demeternity and time as a timeless measure and a temporal measure because it is a necessary condition for a measure to be timeless that the measure be essentially different from time. Even though demeternity has no beginnings and ends *in* it, it is not by virtue of that fact timeless. In short, being *tota simul* or having no beginnings and ends *in* it does *not* characterize demeternity as timeless. Second, as we have just seen, Aquinas holds that while the *being* of demeternal things does not change, demeternal *things* do nevertheless undergo change because they change with respect to such dispositions as place, thoughts, affections and the like. He is also committed to the principle that time measures those things beginning and ending in time. But, then, since changes do occur to demeternal things and those changes are measured by time and occur in time because they begin and end in time, it would appear to follow that the things measured by demeternity are also measured by time and that time and demeternity are *not* mutually exclusive measures. Hence, it follows that demeternal things are temporal things, not atemporal or timeless things, and that demeternity is a measure of temporal things, not a measure of atemporal or timeless things. Indeed, Aquinas himself admits as much and supports this understanding of his account of time and de-meternity when he says in his reply to objection 1 (article 5 of question 10) that demeternal things are measured by demeternity with respect to their natural being, but are measured by time with respect to their display of successiveness, that is, with respect to the successive beginnings and ends marked by the changes that occur to them.

It turns out that demeternity is not timeless and a measure of timeless things and that demeternity and time are not mutually exclusive measures. According to Aquinas' account of time and demeternity the difference between actually having beginnings and ends and not having them but merely being connected to or associated with them does not succeed in distinguishing a timeless measure from a temporal measure. Consequently, the difference between having beginnings and ends *in* it and having no beginnings and ends *in* it does not distinguish a temporal measure from a timeless measure nor does it distinguish two measures as mutually exclusive; and being *tota simul* or having no beginnings and ends *in* it does *not* characterize a measure as timeless and a measure of timeless things.

But the problems with Thomas's comparisons do not end here. There is one more difficulty though this one is not insurmountable and can be overcome by making a relatively minor revision. Recall that for Aquinas eternity does *not* differ in any significant way from time simply on the grounds that eternity has neither a beginning nor an end while time has both a beginning and an end. This difference is only an accidental one on Aquinas' view. Rather, eternity differs in a significant way from time on the grounds that eternity is *tota simul* because it has no before and after or beginnings and ends *in* it while time, on the other hand, is not *tota simul* because it does have before and after or beginnings and ends *in* it. This difference was supposed to be the essential difference between eternity and time and as such was supposed to characterize eternity as timeless and a measure of timeless things on Aquinas' view. However, it has now been shown that, by his own account of time and demeternity, having no beginnings and ends *in* it does not characterize a measure as timeless and a measure of timeless things.

So, in order to sustain his claim that there is an essential difference and not merely an accidental difference between time and eternity by virtue of which eternity is timeless, Aquinas cannot hold that the essential difference between the two consists only in the fact that time has beginnings and ends *in* it while eternity does not. He must say more about the difference between them if he is going to continue to hold that there is an essential difference which makes eternity timeless and, indeed, he does say more. In his comparison of time and demeternity in article 5 of question 10 Thomas says that, unlike demeternity, eternity is in no way even compatible (*neque compatitur*) with before and after or beginnings and ends. The reason he gives for this is that like the being of demeternal things the being of the things measured by eternity is unchangeable, but unlike the being of demeternal things the being of the things measured by eternity cannot even be connected to or associated with (*nec adjunctum*) change-ableness and this follows from his view that unlike demeternal things the things measured by eternity do not undergo any changes of any kind. But, then, if the being of eternal things is unchangeable *and* eternal things have absolutely no beginnings and ends at all because they do not change in any respect whatsoever, it follows that eternal things are not measured by time because time measures only those things beginning and ending in time. So, on his own view, it would be easy for Aquinas to revise his account of the essential difference between time and eternity in such a way that eternity is a measure of things that are *not* also measured by time. He could hold that time and eternity differ essentially by virtue of the fact that the being of temporal things is changeable and temporal things change with respect to other dispositions as well while the being of eternal things is unchangeable and eternal things do *not* change with respect to any other dispositions at all. On this revised account time and eternity would differ essentially and eternity would be timeless and a measure of timeless things because the things measured by eternity would not also be measured by time. If Aquinas would not accept this revised account or one very much like it, then he has failed to characterize any essential difference between eternity and time and on his view eternity turns out to be nothing but endless temporal duration. It is reasonable to think that Aquinas would accept some revision of this kind since it is quite plain from question 10 that on his view eternity is timeless and a measure of timeless things and that things measured by eternity not only have unchangeable being but also do not undergo any other kind of changes whatsoever.

Moreover, it is equally plain from question 8 of the *Summa Theologiae* that on Aquinas' view God is omnipresent. In article 1 of question 8 Aquinas makes it unequivocally clear that on his own view God is in everything as an agent is present to a patient upon which it acts. His reason for claiming that God is in everything in this manner is that God is the causal agent of the existence of all created things and every such agent must be *connected to* or *associated with* (*conjungi*) every patient upon which it acts immediately and it must be in direct *contact with* (*contingere*) every patient through its own power. Aquinas justifies this reason by appealing to the more general principle which he attributes to Aristotle that both the mover and the moved, both the agent and the patient, must exist *simul*, that is, must exist together, and, hence, at the same *time*. So, Thomas is committed to holding that God and any given created thing exist at the same time and in direct contact with one another. He further claims that the existence of created things is the proper effect of God and that this effect in things is caused by God not only when created things first begin to exist, but also for *as long as* they continue to exist. Aquinas concludes from these claims that God is necessarily present to a created thing for as long a *time* as it exists and that not only is God in everything but he is in everything innermostly because existence is innermost and most fundamentally present in all things.

So, from his own account of divine omnipresence it is clear that Aquinas cannot subscribe to the doctrine that God is timeless. On his own view Aquinas is committed to holding that God undergoes changes which occur in time and so he is also committed to holding that God is measured by time. For on his own view God is in each temporal thing, God is in each temporal thing for as long a time as it exists, and God and any given temporal thing exist at the same time. But, then, since the existence of each temporal thing had a beginning and will also have an end, it follows that God's presence in each temporal thing had a beginning and will also have an end. Hence, God changes with respect to being in temporal things. Moreover, since the existence of each temporal thing begins and ends in time, God's presence in each temporal thing begins and ends in time and so the changes that occur to God with respect to being in temporal things are changes which occur to him in time. Consequently, God is measured by time on Aquinas' view of divine omnipresence because God's presence in temporal things begins and ends in time and Aquinas insists that time measures those things beginning and ending in time. It turns out, then, that on Aquinas' own view God is not timeless and, hence, not eternal, if he is omnipresent.

Furthermore, from his own account of divine omnipresence Aquinas is committed to holding that God is in the United Nations Building for as long a time as it exists and that God and the U.N. Building exist at the same time. But since the U.N. Building existed yesterday as well as the day before yesterday, it follows from Aquinas' view that God was in the U.N. Building both yesterday and the day before. So, because this argument holds for God's presence in all temporal things, it further follows that God is continuously measured by time as long as time exists. The result of all this is that the doctrine of divine eternity as timelessness and the doctrine of divine omnipresence as they are enunciated by Thomas do jointly entail a contradiction and the argument with which this discussion began actually does apply to St. Thomas.

NOTES

1. Aquinas follows Boethius by name in claiming that eternity is *tota simul*. The passage referred to by Aquinas occurs in Boethius' *The Consolation of Philosophy,* Book V, prose 6.

2. It is important not to confuse the necessary conditions for being timeless with the necessary conditions for being eternal. On Aquinas' view a measure is essentially different from time and so is timeless if and only if it is *tota simul* and, as we shall see shortly, on his view a measure can be *tota simul* or timeless even if it has both a beginning and an end.

17

Descartes on God's Ability to Do the Logically Impossible

With very few exceptions philosophers believe that no account of the doctrine of divine omnipotence is adequate if it entails that God can do what is logically impossible. Descartes is credited with believing otherwise. In his article "Descartes on the Creation of the Eternal Truths,"[1] Harry Frankfurt attributes to Descartes the belief that God is "a being for whom the logically impossible is possible" (F, 44). In addition, Frankfurt claims that because of this belief Descartes' account of God's omnipotence is open to the charge of being incoherent. I will argue that it is wrong to attribute this belief to Descartes and that if his account of divine omnipotence is incoherent, it is incoherent for reasons other than that it entails the possibility of what is logically impossible.[2]

Interpreting Descartes' view is complicated because his account of God's omnipotence occurs exclusively in his treatment of the unique Cartesian doctrine that God created the eternal truths and this doctrine is not easy to understand. It is not easy to understand because it does not appear in any of Descartes' books and so it is not developed systematically or in any one place, nor do I think that it was ever fully developed even in Descartes' own mind. Instead, his treatment of the doctrine occurs in ten distinct passages written over a period of nineteen years from 1630 to 1649. The passages occur in eight of his Letters[3] (hereafter L) and in

From *Canadian Journal of Philosophy* 14, no. 3 (September 1984): 455–75. Reprinted by permission.

two of his Replies[4] (hereafter R) to the objections to the meditations. These passages are quite brief and in each one the doctrine that God created the eternal truths is discussed in connection with some specific question about his philosophy or some specific question about the doctrine itself. Because the doctrine is developed in this way its more detailed or secondary features are mentioned only randomly and separately and we cannot even be sure that we have a record of all the features of the doctrine that Descartes himself thought to be important. So, in order to determine what Descartes believed about divine omnipotence his view has to be pieced together from his remarks and claims in these ten passages. Nevertheless, I think that he said enough in these passages to determine both the substance of his doctrine about eternal truths and what he believed about God's omnipotence. In chronological order the ten passages are to be found in the following places: 15 April 1630, a letter to Mersenne; 6 May 1630, a letter to Mersenne; 27 May 1630, a letter to Mersenne; 17 May 1638, a letter to Mersenne; August 1641, a letter to the pseudonymous Hyper-aspistes; 1641 or 42, Reply Five; 1641 or 42, Reply Six; 2 May 1644, a letter to Mesland; 29 July 1648, a letter to Arnauld; and 5 February 1649, a letter to More.

The central core of Descartes' doctrine can be stated quite simply. God created the eternal truths. The first formulation of this doctrine occurs in the first letter to Mersenne on the subject (15 April 1630) and provides an initial indication of how the doctrine is to be finally understood.

The mathematical truths which you call eternal have been laid down by God and depend on Him entirely no less than the rest of his creatures. Indeed to say that these truths are independent of God is to talk of Him as if He were Jupiter or Saturn and to subject Him to the Styx and the Fates. Please do not hesitate to assert and proclaim everywhere that it is God who has laid down these laws in nature just as a king lays down laws in his kingdom. There is no single one that we cannot understand if our mind turns to consider it. They are all *inborn in our minds* just as a king would imprint his laws on the hearts of all his subjects if he had enough power to do so. . . .

It will be said that if God had established these truths He could change them as a king changes his laws. To this the answer is: "Yes he can, if his will can change." "But I understand them to be eternal and unchange-able."—"I make the same judgment about God." "But His will is free."—"Yes, but his power is incomprehensible." In general we can assert that God can do everything that we can comprehend but not that he cannot do what we cannot comprehend. It would be rash to think that our imagination reaches as far as His power. (L, 11–12)

In this passage Descartes mentions mathematical truths as an example of eternal truths, but he does not restrict his doctrine to mathematical truths. Examples of geometrical, logical, and moral truths are cited in other passages devoted to this doctrine and in the third letter to Mersenne on the subject (27 May 1630) Descartes makes it clear that the doctrine applies to *all essences* and *all truths* about essences. "For it is certain that he is no less the author of creatures' essence than he is of their existence; and this essence is nothing other than the eternal truths" (L, 14).

Some commentators have held that Descartes acknowledges exceptions to this doctrine, but Frankfurt argues against this view (F, 47–50). What all commentators, including Frankfurt, fail to realize is that this doctrine is an instantiation of a more general doctrine and functions in one of its aspects to show that not even necessary truths are exceptions to the general doctrine. The general doctrine is stated in the passage just cited from the third letter to Mersenne. It is the doctrine that God has created absolutely *everything*. There Descartes claims to know that "God is the author of everything and that these truths are something and consequently that he is their author" (L, 15). Moreover, the doctrine that there is nothing independent of God's creative power is repeated in different ways throughout these ten passages. In the second letter to Mersenne on the subject (6 May 1630) Descartes cautions against holding the view that the eternal truths would be true even if God did not exist because the existence of God is the first and the most eternal of all possible truths and the one from which alone *all others* derive, and he insists that God is the sole author on whom *all things* depend (L, 14). Eleven years later the doctrine is stated in no uncertain terms in Reply Six.

> To one who pays attention to God's immensity, it is clear that nothing at all can exist which does not depend on Him. This is true not only of everything that subsists, but of all order, of every law, and of every reason of truth and goodness; for otherwise God, . . . , would not have been wholly indifferent to the creation of what he has created. For if any reason for what is good had preceded His preordination, it would have determined Him towards that which it was best to bring about; but on the contrary because He determined himself towards those things which ought to be accomplished, for that reason, . . . , *they are very good*; that is to say, the reason for their goodness is the fact that He wished to create them so. (R, 250)

It is clear from all this that Descartes would *not* acknowledge any exceptions to the doctrine that God created the eternal truths because according to his more general doctrine of divine creation God has created literally everything. There are no substances, there are no essences, there are no truths possible or necessary about anything whatsoever that are independent of God, for God *created* them all.

Descartes has good reasons for holding this radical view of divine creation. First, he subscribes to the doctrine of divine independence. As the passage just cited shows, if anything exists that is independent of God, then God would be determined by something independent of him in the creation of what he creates and, hence, God would not be independent of everything else. But "it is clear by the light of nature that there can be only one supreme being independent of everything else" (L, 115). Since it is God that is independent of everything else, it follows from the doctrine of divine independence that there is nothing independent of God. Second, Descartes endorses a strict version of the doctrine of divine simplicity. He steadfastly maintains that willing, understanding, and creating are all identical in God without one being even conceptually prior to the other (L, 15; R, 248). It follows from this understanding of divine simplicity that if something exists which was not created by God, then it is independent of God and determines his creative will. For if anything not created by God preceded an act of his creative will, it would also precede his understanding. Hence, it could not be said to exist in the divine understanding and so it could not be said to be dependent on God. It would follow from this that there is something independent of God which determines his creative will. Since the latter is excluded by the doctrine of divine independence, it follows from these two doctrines and it is the view of creation proposed by Descartes that there is absolutely nothing that was not created by God. God created literally everything, including the eternal truths.

According to Descartes' general doctrine of divine creation God's creative will cannot be determined by any antecedent knowledge of possibilities or goods or truths which he has not already created because there are no possibilities or goods or truths prior to God's creation of them. So, since the more specific doctrine that God created the eternal truths is only an instantiation of the general doctrine that *everything* was created by God, the more specific doctrine entails that God was not determined in his creation of the eternal truths, not even in his creation of the law of contradiction. In his letter to Mesland of 2 May 1644 Descartes acknowledges this entailment with the claim that "God cannot have been determined to make it true that contradictories cannot be true together, and therefore . . . he could have done the opposite" (L, 151). It is this claim which prompts Frankfurt to attribute to Descartes the belief that for God the logically impossible is possible. Frankfurt treats Descartes' claim this way:

> What is troublesome in this claim that God could have made contradictions true is, of course, understanding the "could." The assertion that some state of affairs can be brought about ordinarily entails that that state of affairs is logically possible. Descartes's statement that God could have made contradictions true seems to entail, accordingly, the logical possibility of the logically impossible . . . . That there is a deity with infinite power is supposed by Descartes to entail the possibility of what is logically impossible. (F, 43–44)

In the same passage Frankfurt subsequently characterizes Descartes' notion of God as "the notion of a being for whom the logically impossible is possible."

According to this account we are to believe that Descartes' claim commits him to acknowledging that for God the logically impossible is possible or, more precisely, that for God the negation of the law of contradiction is possible, and we are to believe this because of Frankfurt's principle that the assertion that some state of affairs can be brought about *ordinarily* entails that that state of affairs is logically possible. Unfortunately Frankfurt's account of Descartes' claim is no less troublesome than Descartes' claim itself. The trouble with Frankfurt's account is that there are at least three distinct ways of understanding the statement that for God the negation of the law of contradiction is possible and so there are at least three distinct ways of understanding Frankfurt's account of Descartes' claim. Although these three ways of understanding Frankfurt's account are not mutually exclusive and several of his remarks suggest that he intends his account of Descartes' claim to be understood in all three of these ways, it is necessary to make them explicit and treat them separately if we are to identify the essential elements of Descartes' doctrine that God created the eternal truths.

First, the statement that for God the negation of the law of contradiction is possible can be understood as the assertion that for God the negation of the law of contradiction is *a possibility*, that is, that the negation of the law of contradiction is a possibility God could have chosen to actualize instead of actualizing the law of contradiction. Among other things Frankfurt says, this understanding is suggested by both his principle that the assertion that some state of affairs can be brought about ordinarily entails that that state of affairs is logically possible as well as his claim that on Descartes' account God's "*choices* [italics mine] are in no way submissive to any moral or rational constraints at all" (F, 42). Given this understanding of Frankfurt's account we are to believe that Descartes' claim commits him to acknowledging that the negation of the law of contradiction is a possibility God could have *chosen* to actualize. The difficulty with this account of Descartes' claim is that his claim does *not* entail that the negation of the law of contradiction is a possibility God could have chosen to actualize without some further principle to the effect that God brings about states of affairs by actualizing real and uncreated possibilities. Descartes' claim *and* this principle taken *together* would entail that the negation of the law of contradiction is a possibility God could have chosen to actualize, but Descartes explicitly rejects that principle. On Descartes' view God does not bring something about by first consulting a list of alternative possibilities and then *choosing* one of those possibilities to actualize because, on Descartes' view, there are no possibilities or goods or truths prior to God's creative activity which could determine his creative activity or from which he could choose. In other words, because *nothing* exists prior to God's creative activity the statement that God did bring about some state of affairs (e.g., the existence of the law of contradiction) does *not* entail that that state of affairs (the existence of the law of contradiction) was a possibility prior to the exercise of the divine creative will, nor does the statement that God *could* have brought about some state of affairs (e.g., the existence of the negation of the law of contradiction) entail that that state of affairs (the existence of the negation of the law of contradiction) was a possibility prior to the exercise of the divine creative will. For Descartes God's creative activity does not consist in actualizing real and uncreated possibilities and so the eternal truths were not created out of possibilities. Rather, like everything else the eternal truths were created by God *ex nihilo,* that is, they were created by God and *nothing* preceded their existence out of which they were made. So, Descartes' claim that God could have done the opposite with respect to making it true that contradictories cannot be true together does *not* commit Descartes to acknowledging that the negation of the law of contradiction is a possibility God could have chosen to actualize. On the contrary, Descartes' doctrine that God created the eternal truths entails that the negation of the law of contradiction is *not* a possibility God could have chosen to actualize because according to that doctrine *nothing* exists prior to the exercise of God's creative will.

On a second understanding, the statement that for God the negation of the law of contradiction is possible can be understood as the assertion that God can repeal the law of contradiction and replace it with the negation of the law of contradiction. Even though the negation of the law of contradiction is not a possibility God could have chosen to actualize and the law of contradiction was not created out of anything, God might be able to annul the law of contradiction and create its negation as a substitute. This understanding of Frankfurt's account is supported by his claim that on Descartes' view "the eternal truths are inherently as contingent as any other propositions" (F, 42). Given this second understanding of Frankfurt's account we are to believe that Descartes' claim commits him to acknowledging that God can change the law of contradiction. The difficulty with this account of Descartes' claim is that his claim does *not* entail that God can change the law of contradiction without some further premise to the effect that God can change whatever he does. In other words, Descartes is not committed to acknowledging that God can change the law of contradiction unless he accepts the view that God can change the eternal truths. But Descartes explicitly rejects that view. In his third letter to Mersenne on the subject (27 May 1630) Descartes claims that the eternal truths were created from all eternity (L, 15) and in the passage quoted at the beginning of this discussion from his first letter to Mersenne on the subject (15 April 1630) Descartes himself raises this issue and settles it by making the point that the eternal truths are *eternal* and *unchangeable* because they were established by the will of God which is eternal and unchangeable (L, 11). On Descartes' view the eternal truths were created by God from all eternity and cannot be changed by God, that is, they have no beginning and no end and so they are *coeternal* with God. It follows from this that there is never any time at which the eternal truths do not obtain and this entails that there is never any time at which the law of contradiction does not obtain. So, Descartes' claim that God could have done the opposite with respect to making it true that contradictories cannot be true together does *not* commit him to acknowledging that God can change the law of contradiction in favor of its negation. On the contrary, one of the features of Descartes' doctrine that God created the eternal truths is that God cannot change the eternal truths and this entails that God cannot change the law of contradiction in favor of its negation.

On a third understanding, the statement that for God the negation of the law of contradiction is possible can be understood as the assertion that God can violate the law of contradiction, that is, that God can bring about logically impossible states of affairs. Even though the negation of the law of contradiction is not a possibility God could have chosen to actualize and God cannot change the law of contradiction, God might be able to bring it about, for example, that what was done is undone (i.e., that some past event has not occurred). Frankfurt makes it clear that this is at least in part the way his account is to be understood, for he devotes an entire section of his article to a discussion of logically impossible states of affairs that God is supposed to be able to bring about on his interpretation of Descartes' doctrine (F, 47–50). Given this understanding of Frankfurt's account we are to believe that Descartes' claim commits him to acknowledging that having established the law of contradiction God can violate it by bringing about logically impossible states of affairs. The difficulty with this account of Descartes' claim is that his claim does *not* entail that God can violate the law of contradiction without adding a further premise to the claim. Frankfurt seems to think that he has identified the missing premise when he attributes to Descartes the principle that God's power is unlimited by the law of contradiction (F, 50), a principle which presumably is an instance of the more general principle that God's power is unlimited by the eternal truths. Now while Descartes subscribes to both versions of this principle, what he means by the principle is that God was not *antecedently* determined or limited in his creation of the eternal truths or the law of contradiction because *nothing* existed prior to his creation of them which could have determined or limited him in their creation. In Reply Six Descartes emphasizes this aspect of his doctrine by saying, "God did not will . . . the three angles of a triangle to be equal to two right angles because he knew that they could not be otherwise . . . it is because he willed the three angles of a triangle to be *necessarily* [my italics] equal to two right angles that this is true and cannot be otherwise; and so in other cases" (R, 248). In other words, the principle invoked by Frankfurt does not satisfy the condition required of the missing premise and so conjoined with Descartes' claim it does not commit Descartes to acknowledging that God can violate the law of contradiction. What is required of the missing premise is that it be the assertion of the principle that having established the eternal truths God is not *subsequently* determined or limited by them in the creation of what he creates. It is this principle that Descartes would have to endorse if there is to be any justification at all for this third understanding of Frankfurt's account of Descartes' claim. But Descartes does not endorse this principle. In Reply Five Descartes addresses this issue by saying that

> . . . in the same way as the poets feign that, while the fates were indeed established by Jove, yet once established, he was restricted in his action by his maintenance of them; similarly I do not think that the essence of things, and those mathematical truths which may be known about them, are independent of God; yet I think that because God so wished it and brought it to pass, they *are* immutable and eternal. (R, 226)

The implication here is quite clear. God was not determined or limited in his creation of the eternal truths, but having established them as both eternal and immutable he is restricted in his subsequent actions by his maintenance of them. On Descartes' view the law of contradiction is co-eternal with God and having established it from all eternity God *cannot* subsequently violate it by bringing about logically impossible states of affairs.

Descartes confirms this aspect of his doctrine by citing several con-tradictory things that God cannot do. According to Descartes' claims in Reply Six it is contradictory that accidents should exist independently of substances and so God cannot make real accidents (R, 250); and according to his letter to Hyperaspistes (August 1641) God cannot create beings that can exist independently of him nor can he destroy anything by his positive action (L, 116). Moreover, in his letter to More of 5 February 1649, his last known word on the doctrine that God created the eternal truths, Descartes makes it clear that God *cannot* bring it about that things which have been done are undone and he even gives a definition, not of om-nipotence, but of impotence. There he says, "For we do not take it as a mark of impotence when someone cannot do something we do not understand to be possible, but only when he cannot do something which we distinctly perceive to be possible" (L, 241). This definition has an important consequence. It follows from this definition of impotence that the statement 'God is omnipotent' is not falsified by the claim that there is something he cannot do if *either* we do not understand that thing to be possible *or* we perceive that thing to be altogether impossible (i.e., to be contrary to the law of contradiction). Descartes explicitly makes the point that this is a *consequence* of his definition by saying, "we do not . . . perceive it to be possible for what is done to be undone—on the contrary, we perceive it to be altogether impossible, and so it is no defect of power in God not to do it" (L, 241). According to these passages God cannot violate the law of contradiction and the claim that he cannot does not falsify the statement that God has infinite power. So, Descartes' claim that God could have done the opposite with respect to establishing the law of contradiction does *not* commit him to acknowledging that God can bring about logically impossible states of affairs. On the contrary, one of the features of Descartes' doctrine that God created the eternal truths is that God *cannot* bring about logically impossible states of affairs, that he cannot violate the law of contradiction.

Moreover, Descartes' definition of impotence and its consequence should not lead us to think that on his view what we judge to be altogether impossible or contradictory is due simply to how we perceive things or to the contingent nature of the human mind. Frankfurt attributes this view to Descartes when he characterizes the eternal truths by saying

> The propositions we find to be necessary . . . need not be truths at all. The inconceivability of their falsity . . . is not inherent in them. It is properly to be understood only as relative to the character of our minds. We cannot escape this character, of course, but we *can* realize that God might have made it different from what it is. Since *God is not constrained by the boundaries within which He has enclosed our minds* [my italics], the theoretical limits of human reason must be recognized as *limitations* by which we are bound, rather than as guides to the actual limits of possibility. They are imposed upon us arbitrarily by God's free creation. So, we cannot presume that what we determine to be logically necessary coincides with the ultimate conditions of reality or of truth. The necessities human reason discovers by analysis and demonstration are just necessities of its own contingent nature. In coming to know them, it does not necessarily discover the nature of the world as it is in itself, or as it appears to God." (F, 45)

The difficulty with this characterization of the eternal truths is that it is not at all what Descartes believes. First, Descartes denies that the eternal truths are in any way dependent on the contingent nature of the human mind. In Reply Six he says, "neither should we think *that eternal truths depend upon the human understanding or on other existing things;* they must depend on God alone, who, as the supreme legislator, ordained them from all eternity" (R, 251). Descartes believes that God created the eternal truths from all eternity and that he created them with the properties that they have. It is obvious that he also believes that God created the eternal truths with the property of being necessarily true. Descartes says in several places that the eternal truths are immutable or unchangeable and that God has made them necessarily true.[5] In his letter to Mesland on the subject (2 May 1644) he states quite plainly that contradictories *cannot* be true together and makes it quite clear that the negations of the eternal truths are "things which God could have made possible, but which he in fact wished to make impossible" (L, 151). So, it is wrong to attribute to Descartes the belief that the necessity of the eternal truths is not inherent in them but is, instead, only a function of the human mind. Descartes believes that the eternal truths are necessary because God made them that way.

Second, the belief that the eternal truths determine a boundary which limits or constrains the power of human reason but which does not limit or constrain the power of God is *not* a belief that Descartes holds. As we have already seen, on Descartes' view God created the eternal truths and, having created them from all eternity, he made them eternal, immutable, and necessary. Furthermore, Descartes believes that while God was not determined or necessitated to establish just the set of eternal truths that he did establish (or any at all for that matter), nevertheless, having established that set of eternal truths as logically necessary, he determined himself not to be able to change them or to violate them. So, it is wrong to attribute to Descartes the belief that the power of human reason is limited by the eternal truths while the power of God is not limited by them. Descartes believes that God limited or determined himself by making the eternal truths eternal, immutable, and logically necessary and that it is no defect of power in God not to be able to abrogate the eternal truths.

Third, the notion that the eternal truths do *not* determine "the actual limits of possibility" or "the ultimate conditions of reality or of truth," that there may be some ultimate reality for God unknowable by us and somehow separate or distinct from reality as it appears to us, is simply a fiction and is inconsistent with Descartes' general doctrine of divine creation. On Descartes' view God created everything including the eternal truths. There is no reality or realm of possibility independent of the things created by God and so everything created by God is what constitutes reality for God. Since God created the eternal truths but not their negations, the eternal truths are among the constituents of reality for God but the negations of the eternal truths are *not* among the constituents of reality for God.[6] Moreover, having created the eternal truths as eternal, immutable, and necessary, God made it *impossible* for there to be any conditions that the constituents of reality could satisfy other than those conditions determined by the eternal truths. In other words, the conditions determined by the eternal truths *are* the ultimate conditions of reality and of truth and they establish the actual limits of possibility. So, in coming to know the necessity of the eternal truths by analysis and demonstration what we come to know is reality as it appears to God because there is no other reality, there is nothing else for anyone including God *to* know. For Descartes there is only one reality and it is determined by the eternal truths which were created by God from all eternity. Furthermore, reality as it is known by God is knowable by us. Descartes explicitly addresses this issue in his first letter on the subject of eternal truths, the letter to Mersenne of 15 April 1630. There he says that the eternal truths "are all inborn in our minds" and "there is no single one that we cannot understand if our mind turns to consider it" (L, 11). So, it is wrong to attribute to Descartes the belief that human reason does not discover the nature of reality as it is in itself, or as it appears to God, by coming to know the necessity of the eternal truths through analysis and demonstration. Descartes believes that God created the eternal truths and that they determine the limits of reality and of possibility.

Frankfurt's vision of a reality unintelligible to us and separate from the one we understand is not a part of Descartes' doctrine that God created the eternal truths, nor is that vision entailed by Descartes' doctrine. Rather, that vision is a fiction that results from Frankfurt's failure to recognize Descartes' distinction between what God *could have done* from all eternity with respect to establishing the eternal truths and what God *can do* having established the eternal truths that he did establish. Descartes clearly believes that God created the eternal truths as well as the whole of reality and that having created the eternal truths God cannot now annul, change, violate, or in any other way countermand them. Further, he believes that it is no defect of power in God not to be able to countermand the eternal truths because through his own power *and* will God brought it about both that the eternal truths exist and that he cannot countermand them; that is, Descartes believes that through his own power and will *God determined himself* by creating what he created (R, 250). But Descartes also believes that since there was *nothing* to determine or necessitate God to create what he did create, God could have created a reality different from the one he actually created and so could have determined himself differently. In other words, on Descartes' view God's power must be understood as having two different but related aspects. First, God's power must be understood as being absolute because it is not limited by anything. Nothing exists prior to the exercise of his creative will and so there is *nothing* to determine or limit what he could do. Second, God's power must be understood as being self-determined because he willed it to be limited by something he willed to bring about. By exercising his absolute power to do anything, God willed to bring it about that the law of contradiction and the other eternal truths exist *and* that he cannot override them and so there are things God willed to bring about through his absolute power that determine or limit what he can do and he willed that these things determine or limit what he can do. On Descartes' view God's absolute power is beyond limit or measure because it is prior to anything that could limit it or measure it, while God's self-determined power is limited because it is *measured* by the law of contradiction and the other eternal truths which were freely created by God.

Because he cites only those passages devoted to the claim that God was not determined (that God could have done otherwise) with respect to establishing the eternal truths and ignores the crucial passages in which Descartes develops the idea that God cannot abrogate or countermand the eternal truths, Frankfurt entirely misses Descartes' distinction between God's absolute power and God's self-determined power and so he mistakenly attributes to Descartes the view that God can always do anything. Frankfurt then supposes that, since God can always do anything, God can bring about states of affairs which satisfy conditions distinct from those conditions determined by the eternal truths. From this he concludes that there *are* actual possibilities and ultimate conditions of reality and of truth that are independent of and separate from the eternal truths and so he erroneously attributes two other beliefs to Descartes. One is the belief that the eternal truths do not determine the actual limits of possibility or the ultimate conditions of reality or of truth. The other is the belief that the necessity of the eternal truths is not an ultimate condition of reality or of truth but is only a contingent property of eternal truths which is determined by the contingent nature that the human mind happens to have. So, Descartes is wrongly credited with believing that the necessity of the law of contradiction is simply a function of the contingent nature of the human mind and that the law of contradiction does not govern God's power and does not determine the ultimate conditions of reality or of truth. As a result, Frankfurt mistakenly interprets Descartes as holding the view that the judgments human reason makes about what is logically impossible or contradictory by appealing to the law of contradiction are only a function of the nature of human reason and do not correspond to what is ultimately real or true because the conditions determined by the law of contradiction are not ultimate conditions of reality or of truth, as well as the view that God can do what human reason judges to be logically impossible or contradictory.

In a later attempt to support this interpretation Frankfurt (F, 48–50) cites the three following passages from Descartes:

> I agree that there are contradictions which are so evident, that we cannot put them before our minds without judging them entirely impossible, like the one which you suggest: *that God might have made creatures independent of him.* But if we would know the immensity of his power we should not put these thoughts before our minds. (To Mesland, 2 May 1644, L, 151)

> I do not think that we should ever say of anything that it cannot be brought about by God. For since everything involved in truth and goodness depends on His omnipotence, I would not dare say that God cannot make a mountain without a valley, or that one and two should not be three. I merely say that He has given me such a mind that I cannot conceive a mountain without a valley, or an aggregate of one and two which is not three, and that such things involve a contradiction in my conception. I think the same should be said of a space which is wholly void, or of an extended piece of nothing, or of a limited universe. (To Arnauld, 29 July 1648, L, 236–7)

> For my part, I know that my intellect is finite and God's power is infinite, and so I set no bounds to it; I consider only what I can conceive and what I cannot conceive, and I take great pains that my judgement should accord with my understanding. And so I boldly assert that God can do everything which I conceive to be possible, but I am not so bold as to deny that He can do whatever conflicts with my understanding—I merely say that it involves a contradiction. (To More, 5 February 1649, L, 240–1)

Frankfurt begins his explanation of what he takes to be the significance of these passages by once again contending that "Descartes regards the impossibility of self-contradictory propositions only as a function of the particular character human reason happens to have, rather than as providing us *in any way* [my italics] with a measure of God's power" (F, 48–49). In other words, Frankfurt thinks that in these passages Descartes is propounding two views. First, he thinks that Descartes is propounding the view that the impossibility of self-contradictory propositions is nothing more than a condition of human thought determined by the particular character human reason happens to have rather than an actual condition of reality determined by what is ultimately real or true. Second, he thinks that Descartes is propounding the view that human reason does not *in any way* provide us with a measure of God's power when it judges that certain states of affairs are logically impossible or contradictory by appealing to the law of contradiction *and* its necessity. The difficulty here is that, taken in isolation from the rest of what Descartes has to say about eternal truths, these passages do no more than suggest the bare possibility of Frankfurt's explanation: they do not provide any support for the contention that Descartes actually subscribes to the views Frankfurt is attributing to him. To be sure, Descartes makes some provocative points in these passages, but these points do not separately or jointly entail Frankfurt's explanation and when taken together with the rest of what Descartes has to say about eternal truths they support an interpretation entirely different from Frankfurt's.

Descartes' first provocative point is that God has given him such a mind that he cannot conceive certain contradictory states of affairs such as a mountain without a valley or an aggregate of one and two which is not three. But this does not entail that the impossibility of self-contradictory propositions, and, hence, the necessity of the law of contradiction, are not actual conditions of reality but only conditions of human thought. Even when taken in isolation from the rest of what Descartes has to say about eternal truths, this point is open to an interpretation quite different from Frankfurt's. If God created reality in such a way that there were no conditions for the constituents of reality to satisfy except the conditions determined by the law of contradiction and the other eternal truths, then the *impossibility* of self-contradictory propositions and the *necessity* of the law of contradiction would be determined by what is ultimately real and true and not by the particular character human reason happens to have. Under these circumstances, when human reason judges that self-contradictory propositions are impossible by appealing to the law of contradiction *and* its necessity, those judgments of human reason would be determined by what is ultimately real and true. In other words, the particular character human reason happens to have as well as the impossibility of self-contradictory propositions and the necessity of the law of contradiction would all be determined by the ultimate conditions of reality and truth. So, Descartes' claim that God has given him such a mind that he cannot conceive certain contradictory states of affairs is perfectly compatible with the belief that self-contradictory propositions and contradictory states of affairs are actually logically impossible, and it is perfectly compatible with the belief that the necessity of the law of contradiction is an ultimate condition of reality and of truth and not simply a condition of human thought.

When we consider Descartes' claim about the kind of mind God has given him in conjunction with the rest of what he has to say about eternal truths, it is quite obvious that he does not subscribe to the view that logical necessity is dependent on the human mind. As we have already seen, in Reply Six Descartes explicitly denies that the law of contradiction and the other eternal truths depend upon the human understanding or on other existing things. Instead, he holds, they must depend on God alone who ordained them from all eternity. Descartes also makes it equally clear in other passages already cited in this discussion that on his view God made the law of contradiction and the other eternal truths logically necessary. What Descartes actually believes is that the necessity of the law of contradiction is an ultimate condition of reality and of truth and that the impossibility of self-contradictory propositions is determined by the law of contradiction, not by the particular character human reason happens to have. In fact, according to his view the particular character human reason happens to have is itself determined by the law of contradiction because he holds the view that the structure of reality and the character of all its constituents are determined by the law of contradiction and the other eternal truths which were created by God from all eternity. On Descartes' view he cannot judge that self-contradictory propositions are possible or conceive that contradictory states of affairs could obtain because God has given him such a mind that his judgments about self-contradictory propositions and contradictory states of affairs are determined by the law of contradiction, and the law of contradiction determines that what is asserted by self-contradictory propositions is impossible and that contradictory states of affairs are logically impossible and cannot conceivably obtain. So, Descartes' claim that God has given him such a mind that he cannot conceive certain contradictory states of affairs does not justify attributing to him the belief that the impossibility of self-contradictory propositions is dependent on the human mind and is not an ultimate condition of reality or of truth.

Descartes' second provocative point is made in both the second and third of the three passages quoted above. It is the point that he would not dare say or be so bold as to claim that God cannot do what he judges to be inconceivable or what conflicts with his understanding, but that he can merely say of these things that they involve a contradiction.

However, this does not entail the view Frankfurt attributes to Descartes. It does not entail that human reason does not provide us *in any way* with a measure of God's power when it judges certain things to be logically impossible or contradictory by appealing to the law of contradiction and its necessity. Even when taken in isolation from the rest of what Descartes has to say about eternal truths, the very locutions Descartes uses to make this point suggest an interpretation quite different from the one offered by Frankfurt. At the conclusion of his account of these passages Frankfurt characterizes Descartes' second point by saying that "Descartes openly reaffirms, quite unequivocally, his doctrine that God's power is unlimited by the principle of contradiction" (F, 50). The problem with Frankfurt's reading of these passages is that Descartes does *not* say or affirm, unequivocally or otherwise, that God's power is unlimited by the law of contradiction or that God can do what human reason judges to be logically impossible or contradictory. In fact, the claim that God can violate the law of contradiction or do what human reason judges to be logically impossible or contradictory is conspicuous by its very absence. It is an easy enough claim to make yet Descartes chooses his words very carefully and quite obviously avoids making that claim. A more obvious interpretation than Frankfurt's is that Descartes does not want to say *either* that God *cannot* do what human reason judges to be logically impossible or contradictory *or* that God *can* do what human reason judges to be logically impossible or contradictory. This suggests that saying these things without qualification is misleading and that from different points of view God's power can be described by saying both, but is misdescribed by saying just one. Descartes' second point in these passages, even when they are taken by themselves, suggests that on his view God's power has two distinct but related aspects. It suggests that from one point of view God's power is unlimited by the law of contradiction and the other eternal truths while from another point of view God's power is *not* unlimited by the law of contradiction and the other eternal truths, and so it suggests that by appealing to the law of contradiction and its necessity human reason provides us with a measure of God's power in one of its aspects.

When we take into account everything Descartes says about eternal truths it is obvious that in these passages he has not simply omitted or overlooked saying that God can do what is logically impossible or what human reason judges to be contradictory. In several different passages already cited in this discussion Descartes makes it abundantly clear that on his view God *cannot* do what is logically impossible, or what human reason judges to be self-contradictory by appealing to the law of contradiction, and the claim that he cannot does not falsify the claim that God has infinite power. Descartes believes exactly what is suggested in these three passages when he clearly *refuses* to say that God *can* do what human reason judges to be logically impossible or contradictory. He believes that although God was not necessitated or in any other way determined to create the law of contradiction and could have done otherwise, having created the law of contradiction as an ultimate condition of reality and truth, God brought it about that contradictory states of affairs are logically impossible and so God brought it about that it is logically impossible for him to bring about contradictory states of affairs. In other words, Descartes believes that, since God brought it about that he cannot abrogate or in any other way countermand the law of contradiction, the judgments which human reason makes by appealing to the law of contradiction provides us *in one way* with a measure of God's power. They provide us with a measure of God's self-determined power. Because God created the law of contradiction as an ultimate condition of reality and of truth, he cannot bring about logically impossible states of affairs and the judgment that he cannot is a judgment about what is ultimately real and true with respect to his self-determined power.

But Descartes also believes that because God's power is absolute in one of its aspects, that because God was not necessitated or in any other way determined to create what he did create and could have done otherwise, we should not say or entertain the thought that God cannot do what human reason judges to be logically impossible. On Descartes' view, we should refrain from saying or thinking this *not* because God *can* do what human reason judges to be logically impossible and we would be wrong in saying or thinking it, but because we can be seriously misled in our thinking about God's power if we understand *only* that God cannot do what human reason judges to be logically impossible. First, we can be misled into thinking that there is something independent of God which determines or limits his power when the truth is that God's power, while determined, is self-determined by the free use of his absolute and undetermined power. God himself, not something else, brought it about that he cannot abrogate or in any other way countermand the law of contradiction. So, if we understand only that God cannot do what human reason judges to be logically impossible, then we will not know the immensity of God's power because we will not understand that it is God himself who brought it about that he cannot do what is logically impossible. Second, if we understand only that God cannot do what human reason judges to be logically impossible we can be misled into thinking that we thereby comprehend the power of God when the truth is that God's power is incomprehensible.[7] Both God's power and human reason are determined by the law of contradiction which God established from all eternity as an ultimate condition of reality and of truth, but, since God could have done otherwise with respect to establishing the law of contradiction, the ultimate conditions of reality and of truth could have been different and so both God's power and human reason could have been determined differently by God. God could have created in such a way that things would not be logically impossible that are now logically impossible and that human reason would not judge things to be logically impossible that it now judges to be logically impossible. But while we can know *that* God could have created differently, the power of God is incomprehensible because we cannot understand *how* it could be that God could have created differently. We cannot understand this because human understanding is determined by the ultimate conditions of reality and of truth. For example, we understand that contradictory states of affairs cannot obtain because God established the law of contradiction as an ultimate condition of reality and of truth and, as an ultimate condition of reality and of truth, the law of contradiction determines human understanding with respect to contradictory states of affairs. On the other hand, if we understood how it could be that God could have done differently with respect to establishing the law of contradiction, then we would understand that contradictory states of affairs *can* obtain, and if we understood the latter, then it would have to be an ultimate condition of reality and of truth that the law of contradiction does *not* obtain because human understanding is determined by the ultimate conditions of reality and of truth. But, since God established the law of contradiction as an ultimate condition of reality and of truth, it is not an ultimate condition of reality and of truth that the law of contradiction does not obtain, and so we cannot understand how it could be that God could have done differently with respect to establishing the law of contradiction. In other words, the condition required for understanding how it could be that God could have done differently with respect to establishing the law of contradiction does not obtain and it would obtain if and only if God had actually done differently with respect to establishing the law of contradiction and so we could understand how it is that God could have done differently if and only if God *had* done differently. On Descartes' view, the power of God is incomprehensible because God could have done differently with respect to establishing the law of contradiction and we cannot understand how it could be that he could have done differently. So, if we understand only that God cannot do what human reason judges to be logically impossible, then we will not know the immensity of God's power because we will not know that he could have created differently and that his power is thereby incomprehensible.

Descartes' caution against saying or thinking that God cannot do what human reason judges to be logically impossible is not a caution against saying or thinking what is false. It is not an oblique way of claiming that God can do what is logically impossible. Instead, it is a caution against saying or thinking that God's power is determined by something independent of him rather than that his power is self-determined and absolute, and it is a caution against overlooking the fact that God's power is incomprehensible, that God created the law of contradiction and could have done otherwise. So, Descartes' second provocative point that he would not dare say or be so bold as to claim that God cannot do what human reason judges to be logically impossible *does not* justify attributing to him the belief that human reason does not in any way provide us with a measure of God's power when it judges certain things to be impossible or contradictory by appealing to the necessity of the law of contradiction. In short, these three passages cited by Frankfurt do not support his interpretation. They do not support his contention that Descartes regards the impossibility of self-contradictory propositions only as a function of the particular character human reason happens to have rather than as providing us in any way with a measure of God's power, nor do they support his notion that Descartes embraces the doctrine that God's power is unlimited by the principle of contradiction.

The result of all this is that Frankfurt's account of Descartes' doctrine is wrong. Descartes' claim that God could have done the opposite with respect to establishing the law of contradiction was not intended to entail, nor does it actually entail, the statement that for God the negation of the law of contradiction is possible. Descartes' claim does not entail that statement under any of the three distinct ways of understanding the statement. But not only is it the case that this entailment does *not* hold, it follows from Descartes' doctrine of divine creation that the negation of the law of contradiction is *not* a possibility God could have actualized, that God *cannot* change the law of contradiction in favor of its negation, and that God *cannot* violate the law of contradiction by bringing about logically impossible states of affairs. In other words, Descartes' doctrine entails that God *cannot* do what is logically impossible and his claim that God could have done the opposite with respect to establishing the law of contradiction does not itself entail the contrary. So, Descartes' doctrine that God created the eternal truths provides no justification at all for attributing to him the belief that God can do what is logically impossible and if his account of divine omnipotence is incoherent, it is incoherent for reasons other than that it entails the possibility of what is logically impossible.

NOTES

1. Harry Frankfurt, "Descartes on the Creation of the Eternal Truths," *The Philosophical Review* 86 (1977): 36–57. In what follows, this article is referred to as K.

2. There are others who attribute such a belief to Descartes. In his article "Descartes, Mathematics, and God" (*The Philosophical Review* 66 [1957]), Leonard G. Miller holds it to be a consequence of Descartes' account of omnipotence that, "the denial of an allegedly necessary truth really is not inconceivable and really is not self-contradictory" (p. 463). Peter Geach, in an article titled "Omnipotence" (*Philosophy* 48, [1973]), credits Descartes with deliberately adopting and defending the doctrine that ". . . God can do everything absolutely: everything that can be expressed in a string of words that makes sense; even if that sense can be shown to be self-contradictory, God is not bound in action, as we are in thought, by the laws of logic" (p. 9). More recently in *Does God Have a Nature?* (Milwaukee: Marquette University Press, 1980) Alvin Plantinga credits Descartes with teaching that, "there are no necessary truths at all; every truth is contingent" (p. 102). The account of Descartes' doctrine of divine omnipotence given by these commentators is not as detailed as the account given by Frankfurt, but these commentators make some of the same crucial errors of interpretation made by Frankfurt.

3. *Descartes—Philosophical Letters*, trans. and ed. by Anthony Kenny (Oxford: Clarendon Press, 1970). In what follows, this book is referred to as L.

4. *The Philosophical Works of Descartes*, trans. by Elizabeth S. Haldane and G. R. T. Ross, Vol. II (New York: Dover Publications, 1955). In what follows, this book is referred to as R.

5. See Reply Five, R, 226; Reply Five, R, 227; Reply Six, R, 248; Letter to Mersenne, 15 April 1630, L, 11; and Letter to Mesland, 2 May 1644, L, 151.

6. To be sure the *propositions* asserting the negations of the eternal truths are among the constituents of reality for God, but the negations of the eternal truths are not *themselves* among the constituents of reality for God, i.e., the nega-

tions of the eternal truths are not themselves truths or even possible truths.

7. For Descartes' remarks on the incomprehensibility of God and his power see the letter to Mersenne, 15 April 1630, L, 12; the letter to Mersenne, 27 May 1630, L, 15; and Reply Five, R, 218.

18

The Paradox of Eden

In the book of Genesis we are told that God created Adam and Eve and put them in the garden of Eden. God also placed in the midst of the garden of Eden the tree of the knowledge of good and evil. Adam and Eve were permitted to eat of any of the trees in the garden of Eden, but God commanded them not to eat the fruit of the tree of the knowledge of good and evil. The forbidden fruit was eaten by Adam and Eve and God punished them for their disobedience (see Genesis 3:16–19).

Notice that there is a difficulty with this story. Before they ate the forbidden fruit Adam and Eve either knew that obeying God is good and disobeying God is evil or they did not know this. If they knew it, then Adam and Eve would have already possessed the knowledge of good and evil and through his omniscience God would know this and he would also know that Adam and Eve would not very likely be tempted to eat the forbidden fruit because they would have nothing to gain by disobeying God. So, since God's command not to eat the fruit of the tree of the knowledge of good and evil was an inadequate and unfair test of the righteousness of Adam and Eve if they already possessed the knowledge of good and evil, God acted unjustly by making this command if they already had this knowledge.

On the other hand, if Adam and Eve did *not* know that obeying God is good and disobeying God is evil, then they could not have known

From *International Journal for Philosophy of Religion* 15 (1984): 171. Reprinted by permission.

that it was wrong or evil to eat the fruit of the tree of the knowledge of good and evil. So, since God punished Adam and Eve for doing something that they could not have known to be wrong or evil, God acted unjustly by punishing them. It would appear to follow that whether or not Adam and Eve knew that obeying God is good and disobeying God is evil, God acted unjustly. But, then, God is just at one time and unjust at another time. Consequently, being just is *not* a necessary or essential property of God.

19

Divine Omniprescience:
Can an Effect Precede Its Cause?

The belief that God is omniscient with respect to the future, that God knows *everything* that will ever occur, is what I refer to as the doctrine of divine omniprescience. For all anyone really knows it might be possible for that doctrine to be true. Indeed, it might be logically possible that God exists and that he is omniprescient, immutable, and the preexisting creator of the universe. Perhaps, too, it is logically possible that God is *not* eternal, that is, that God began to exist. If these things are actually logically possible and if an author does in fact bring about the existence of the compositions he writes, as so many seem to think, then it would appear to be true that an effect can precede its cause. Consider the following observations and assumptions.

Notice first that it is quite plainly true that there exists an enormous multitude of compositions. By a composition I mean such a thing as a play, a poem, a story, an essay, a novel, a review, and the like. Though there is a difference in kind, it is no less certain that Shaw's play, *Pygmalion,* exists than it is that the sun exists. Even though compositions are these days usually recorded in some way, the existence of a composition does not depend upon its being mechanically preserved. Before the advent of printing and before the practice of keeping written records there was an oral tradition for transmitting and preserving compositions such as plays, tales, songs, poems, and even philosophical and religious treatises. It is no less certain that prehistorical compositions once existed than it is that historical compositions now exist or once existed. One sufficient condition for the existence of a composition is the existence of a written or otherwise recorded copy of it, but the existence of a recorded copy of a composition is not a necessary condition for the existence of a composition nor is it the only sufficient condition. There are other conditions that are necessary and, it would appear, sufficient for the existence of a composition.

Surely a composition does exist, whether or not it is mechanically recorded, if it is possible for some sentient being to recite all the lines of the composition, to make an aesthetic critique of it, to provide a grammatical critique of it, to repunctuate it or substitute one word for another in it, to describe its content, to enumerate in their proper order every word and symbol that occurs in it, and, in the case of compositions like plays, to stage the composition. If it is possible for someone to do these things and others like them then it seems quite clear that the composition in question *does exist.* If someone now composes a play or poem in his mind, whether or not he records it and whether or not anyone else knows that he has composed it, it is possible for someone to do the things and others like them mentioned above and, hence, the composition does in fact exist. But if the possibility for someone to do these and other like things for some given composition entails that the composition exists, then some effects do actually occur prior to their causes, given the truth of certain assumptions.

Assume first that God does exist and that even though he is *not* eternal he is omniprescient, immutable, and the pre-existing creator of the universe. Assume second that George Bernard Shaw brought about the existence of the play, *Pygmalion,* by means of a certain sequence of his composing activities which occurred in 1912 or thereabouts. By the first assumption God knows *at every moment* of his existence everything that will ever occur in the future and so before the creation of the universe God knew such things as that he would create the universe, that in the year 1856 George Bernard Shaw would be born, that Shaw would become a prominent Socialist, that Shaw would be awarded the Nobel prize for literature, and so on. By the second assumption, included among the countless numbers of things God knew before the creation of the universe was that by means of a certain sequence of his composing activities which would occur in the year 1912 Shaw would bring about the existence of a play that would be called *Pygmalion.* In addition, God knew what the first word of the play would be and that it would be first, what the second word of the play would be and that it would be second, and what each succeeding word or symbol of the play would be and its proper sequential order; and God knew all this before the creation of the universe. So, before the creation of the universe it was possible for God to recite all the lines of *Pygmalion,* to make an aesthetic critique of *Pygmalion,* to provide a grammatical critique of *Pygmalion,* to enumerate in their proper order every word and symbol that occurs in *Pygmalion,* and so on. It was even possible before the creation of the universe for God to stage the play (he could have prompted his angels in their lines or he could have created some beings for the express purpose of producing *Pygmalion*). In short, since it is possible for someone to do the sort of things enumerated above for some given composition only if that composition already exists, it follows from the two assumptions that *Pygmalion* existed before the creation of the universe.

But *Pygmalion* existed before the creation of the universe only because God knew before creation that Shaw *would* bring about its existence by means of a certain sequence of his composing activities that *would* occur in 1912. Furthermore, God knew those things before creation only because Shaw *did* bring about its existence by means of his composing activity that *did* occur in 1912. It follows from this that *Pygmalion* existed before the creation of the universe only because Shaw brought about its existence by means of his composing activity that occurred in 1912.

Thus, in 1912 Shaw brought about the existence of a composition that began to exist before the creation of the universe and so the coming into existence of *Pygmalion* was an event which occurred prior to the events that caused it to occur. Since the above argument can be generalized to apply to all compositions, it follows from the two assumptions that the coming into existence of any composition is an event which occurs prior to the events that cause it to occur and that there are in fact many effects that are preceded by their causes.

The final result is that an effect can precede its cause if it is true that an author brings about the existence of the compositions he writes and if it is logically possible that God exists and that even though he is not eternal he is omniprescient, immutable, and the preexisting creator of the universe.

20

Metatheism

Theism, atheism, and agnosticism are doctrines about the existence of God. These three doctrines can be characterized by indicating the knowledge claim that is made by the proponents of each doctrine about the truth value of the sentence 'God exists.' The proponents of theism claim to know that the sentence is true, the proponents of atheism claim to know that the sentence is false, and the proponents of agnosticism claim to know that the sentence is either true or false but indeterminate.

Except for those who can be characterized as genuine nonbelievers completely indifferent to questions and claims about the sentence 'God exists,' these three doctrines are ordinarily thought to be exhaustive of the possible views about the existence of God. They are thought to be exhaustive because it is ordinarily thought that these three doctrines exhaustively represent the knowledge claims that are possible about the truth value of the sentence 'God exists.' But they are not exhaustive, there is another possible knowledge claim. One could claim to know that the sentence is neither true nor false. Indeed, this was the claim of the logical positivists and that claim failed and was abandoned because the meaning criterion of the logical positivists failed and was abandoned.

Unfortunately, a perfectly legitimate question was abandoned with logical positivism and that is the question about whether or not some

This paper was written during a sabbatical leave from SUNY College at Buffalo for the academic year 1989–1990. The paper was also presented to the Philosophy Department Staff Symposium at the SUNY College at Fredonia where helpful comments caused me to improve the discussion.

given sentence, 'God exists' for example, is meaningful. In order to raise the question about the meaningfulness of a sentence one need not hold that it is meaningless. It seems perfectly respectable to ask of any given sentence whether or not it is meaningful and if it is what it means. Having been told the meaning of a sentence and understanding it, one may then be in a position to say that it is either true or false and, depending on the actual meaning, may be able to judge that it is in fact true or that it is in fact false. In the last analysis, if no meaning is suggested for some given sentence then one might reasonably conclude that the sentence is neither true nor false. What is being proposed here is not some *general* meaning criterion for the meaningfulness of *all* sentences, but, rather, that it is justifiable to ask questions about the meaningfulness and meaning of any given sentence, for example, the sentence 'God exists.'

So, there is a fourth view about the existence of God which I call metatheism. Atheism and agnosticism can be regarded as coming *after* theism because theists first claim to know that God exists and thereby elicit the responses of atheists and agnostics. Similarly, metatheism comes *after* theism, atheism, and agnosticism because the proponents of these three doctrines first make knowledge claims about the truth value of the sentence 'God exists' and thereby elicit the response of the metatheist.

Metatheism begins with the reasonable supposition that everyone who makes a knowledge claim about the truth value of a sentence must know something about that sentence unless it is logically true or logically false. Either they must know and understand what it means, or they must know that it is meaningful by ultimately relying on the authority of someone who, by virtue of some special expertise, does understand the sentence and does know what it means. For example, as I write this I have actually forgotten the meaning of the sentence '$E=mc^2$,' but I know that it is true. My knowledge claim is based *not* on the fact that I know and understand the meaning of that sentence, but, rather, on the fact that physicists, people with a special expertise, purport to know both the meaning of that sentence and that it is true. Since physicists are among the authorities recognized as providing reliable accounts, my claim to know that the sentence is true is not groundless or inappropriate. On the other hand, I can make no knowledge claim about the truth value of the sentence '$S=fg^2$' unless I either assign some meaning to it, am told its meaning by someone else and understand the meaning, or am told that it is meaningful and true or false by someone whose special expertise can be depended upon to make the account reliable.

Accordingly, the metatheist holds that theism, atheism, and agnosticism are doctrines about the existence of God that share a common assumption. The assumption they share is that the sentence 'God exists' is meaningful, that its meaning is knowable, and that its meaning is or has been known by someone who is or has been an authority by virtue of some special expertise. Since a metatheist does not recognize any authority whose assurance would be judged as reliable for accepting the view that the sentence 'God exists' is meaningful, the metatheist is not prepared to make a judgment about the truth value of that sentence. The metatheist cannot make a judgment about the truth value of the sentence 'God exists' because the metatheist does not know and is not told by theists, atheists, or agnostics what that sentence means. For the metatheist the problem of knowing the meaning of the sentence 'God exists' is prior to the problem of making a judgment about the truth value of that sentence. From the metatheistic point of view theism, atheism, and agnosticism are equally untenable doctrines because they all rest on a highly problematic assumption about the meaning of the sentence 'God exists.' Put quite simply, then, metatheism is the view whose proponents want to know what the sentence 'God exists' means. Metatheism is the doctrine that the meaning of the sentence 'God exists' needs to be stated and explicated and not simply assumed.

It should be quite obvious that if theists, atheists, or agnostics were to reveal the meaning of the sentence 'God exists' in such a way that it could be understood by the average person, then the assumption that the sentence has a knowable meaning would be justified by being stated and explicated. With an explicit understandable meaning stated for the sentence, the metatheist would be prepared to say that the sentence is either true or false and, depending on the actual meaning, might be able to say that it is in fact true or that it is in fact false. But theists, atheists, and agnostics never do in fact state explicitly and completely what the sentence 'God exists' means and it is not at all clear that they all mean the same thing.

In fact, there are good grounds for thinking that the sentence 'God exists' has no common meaning for theists, atheists, and agnostics if, indeed, it does have a clearly understandable meaning for any of them. One reason for thinking this way is that there are claims made by different theists that justify the view that the sentence 'God exists' has no common meaning even for all theists. For example, traditional Judaeo-Christian theists like Augustine and Aquinas hold that God is the greatest possible good and that the good things in creation get their goodness *from* God.[1] On the other hand, modern possible-world theists, under the influence of the possible world semanticists, deny that God is the greatest possible good. They hold that the existence of God and the existence of one good single-celled object would be a conjunctive state of affairs which would be a greater good than the state of affairs that would obtain if God alone existed.[2] This difference between the traditional theists and the modern possible-world theists can be quite fairly characterized by saying that if they were to address the question about what it is that the sentence 'God exists' means, they would each endorse entirely different meanings for that sentence. In other words, traditional theists would maintain that 'the greatest possible good exists' is at least part of the meaning of the sentence 'God exists,' while modern possible-world theists would deny that this is even a part of the meaning of the sentence 'God exists.'

Now, if traditional theists were to elicit the response from some group that the sentence 'God exists' is false, given the traditional theist's partial meaning for that sentence, and if the possible-world theists were to elicit the response from another group that the sentence 'God exists' is false, given the possible-world theist's partial meaning for that sentence, then traditional theists and possible-world theists would both have their own counterpart atheists and, obviously, perhaps their own counterpart agnostics. It is even possible that one could be an atheist *and*, at the same time, a theist or an agnostic.

This kind of dualism is possible for two reasons. First, as we have already seen, the sentence 'God exists' has no meaning that is common to *all* theists. One could be, for example, an atheist with respect to the views of traditional theism and a theist or an agnostic with respect to the views of possible-world theism. Second, atheism and agnosticism are parasitic on theism. They are parasitic on theism in the sense that *after* theists announce the truth of the sentence 'God exists,' atheists and agnostics respond by making their own claims about the truth value of that sentence and those claims *appear* to be relative to whatever explicit understandable meaning, if any, is being assigned by the theists to the sentence 'God exists.' What is not clear in all this is whether or not theists do in fact have an explicit understandable meaning in mind for the sentence 'God exists' and, if they do, whether or not atheists and agnostics are aware of *that* meaning or have *their own* meaning in mind instead, or even *none at all*, when they *appear* to be responding to theists. In cases where atheists have a meaning in mind that is in fact different from the theists to whom they *appear* to be responding, one could be an atheist with respect to the meaning of the atheists and a theist or an agnostic with respect to the meaning of the theists. It should be manifest, then, that one could be an atheist and, at the same time, a theist or agnostic because the sentence 'God exists' has no common meaning for theists, atheists, and agnostics, if, indeed, it does have a clearly understandable meaning for any of them.

So, since the proponents of theism, atheism, and agnosticism never do actually state an explicit understandable meaning for the sentence 'God exists,' the proponents of metatheism do not immediately engage in the enterprise of attempting to make a judgment about the truth value of that sentence. Instead, the metatheist undertakes an entirely different enterprise. The enterprise of the metatheist begins by accepting the assumption of theists, atheists, and agnostics that the sentence 'God exists' is meaningful, that is, that it has an explicit understandable meaning that can be known and stated. The second step in the metatheist's enterprise is to attempt to *discover* or *uncover* the assumed meaning of the sentence 'God exists.' Finally, the metatheist attempts to examine what has been discovered about the meaning of the sentence 'God exists' for the purposes of establishing some ground for making a judgment about the truth value of that sentence.

The most crucial step of the metatheist's enterprise is the second step of attempting to *discover* or *uncover* the assumed meaning of the sentence 'God exists.' This is the most crucial step because one needs to know where to look. It is the view of the metatheist that one must turn to the theists for the purposes of implementing the second step of the metatheistic enterprise. There are two reasons for turning to the theists. First, as we have already observed, atheism and agnosticism are essentially parasitic on theism in the sense that *after* theists announce the truth of the sentence 'God exists,' atheists and agnostics respond by making their own claims about the truth value of that sentence and those claims *appear* to be relative to whatever explicit understandable meaning, if any, is being assigned by *theists* to the sentence 'God exists.' Second, if the claims of atheists and agnostics are not relative to whatever explicit understandable meaning is being assigned by *theists* to the sentence 'God exists,' then their claims are not counterclaims to theism and their claims are irrelevant to the claim of *theists* that the sentence 'God exists' is true. So, the second step in the metatheist's enterprise is to attempt to *discover* or *uncover* the assumed meaning of the sentence 'God exists' by examining theistic writings and claims about God.

Although theists never provide an explicit understandable meaning for the sentence 'God exists' and, hence, never address the central question of metatheism, much has been written by theists about God and God's properties. So, the metatheist is willing to substitute another question for the original question about the meaning of that sentence. The metatheist is willing to address the question: What is God? By examining what theists claim about the nature of God and God's properties, the metatheist is able to make some advances toward the second step in the metatheistic enterprise of discovering or uncovering the assumed meaning of the sentence 'God exists.'

For example, in an effort to explicate the nature of God and to say what God is, some theists have claimed that God has the property of being omnipotent, the property of being omniscient, and the property of being omnibenevolent. This claim can be understood and is construed by the metatheist as a partial explication of the meaning of the sentence 'God exists.' The claim of theists that God exists and has the property of being omnipotent, the property of being omniscient, and the property of being omnibenevolent is understood by the metatheist to entail that 'an omnipotent, omniscient, and omnibenevolent being exists' is at least part of the meaning of the sentence 'God exists.' So, when theists make claims about the nature of God and God's properties in an effort to explicate what God is, metatheists are willing to consider such claims. Metatheists are willing to consider these sorts of claims because, in order to make progress toward understanding the meaning of the sentence 'God exists,' the metatheist must consider statements made by theists that can be construed as providing at least part of the meaning of that sentence.

Nevertheless, the metatheist's enterprise is more complicated than would first appear and there are at least three complications. The first complication is that the sentence 'God exists' has no common meaning even for all theists, as was noted above. The result of this fact is that when several theists assign distinctly different meanings to the sentence 'God exists' the second and third steps of the metatheist's enterprise must be repeated for each of those distinct meanings.

The second complication is that it is always possible that two theists have in fact assigned distinctly different *meanings* to the sentence that they both identify as part of the meaning of the sentence 'God exists.' Upon an initial examination, it might superficially appear that some common partial meaning is being assigned to the sentence 'God exists' by two proponents of apparently identical theistic doctrines. In spite of appearances, however, it may very well be the case that one of the two theists in question does *not* endorse the particular explication given by the other theist for the partial meaning of the sentence 'God exists' that appears to be common to both of them.

For example, in an effort to say what God is, two traditional theists may agree that God is eternal and that God is omnipresent or, from a metatheist's point of view, they may agree that 'an eternal and omnipresent being exists' is at least part of the meaning of the sentence 'God exists.' In spite of this agreement, however, one of the theists might very well subscribe to a philosophical account of the concepts of eternality and omnipresence that the second theist does not actually endorse or is not committed to endorsing. If it were the case that a philosophical account of the concepts of eternality and omnipresence was endorsed by one traditional theist and not endorsed by a second traditional theist, then the first theist and the second theist would have entirely different meanings for the sentence 'an eternal and omnipresent being exists' and, hence, for the sentence 'God exists.' This would be the case even though both of these theists might superficially appear to be 'traditional theists.'

The result of all this is that a critical judgment made by a metatheist about the first theist would be entirely irrelevant to any critical assessment of the second theist, if the critical judgment about the first theist was based on the philosophical account provided by the first theist for the concepts of eternality and omnipresence not endorsed by the second theist. Having applied the second step of the metatheistic enterprise to the claims of the first theist, the metatheist might judge that the sentence 'God exists' is false by virtue of the meaning assigned by the first theist to the sentence 'an eternal and omnipresent being exists.' At the same time, the metatheist might recognize that no judgment about the truth value of the sentence 'God exists' can be made with respect to the claims of the second theist unless the second step of the metatheistic enterprise is applied to the different meaning assigned by the second theist to the sentence 'an eternal and omnipresent being exists.' Since it is always possible for the proponents of apparently identical theistic doctrines to differ on the philosophical account that is found to be acceptable for certain crucial concepts, it is always possible for different theists to have distinctly different meanings for the sentence that they both identify as part of the meaning of the sentence 'God exists.' It is a consequence of possibilities like this that the second and third step of the metatheistic enterprise must be repeated for each distinct meaning that it is possible to identify for the sentence that appears to be commonly regarded by two or more theists as a part of the meaning of the sentence 'God exists.'

The third complication is that some theists might be able to obviate difficulties with their stated view. Some theists might be prepared to reconsider the relevant crucial concepts involved in their view and substitute a new philosophical account of them for the original philosophical account that determined the problematic meaning of the sentence that they identified as part of the meaning of the sentence 'God exists.' In other words, some theists may be able to consistently modify the original meaning they assigned to the sentence that they identify as a part of the meaning of the sentence 'God exists' in favor of a new meaning. For example, the first theist mentioned above might be willing to substitute a new philosophical account of the concepts of eternality and omnipresence and abandon the previously endorsed account of those concepts that originally prompted the metatheist to judge that the sentence 'God exists' is false for the first theist. In such a case as this the first theist would have overcome the objection of the metatheist by modifying the philosophical account of the relevant crucial concepts and would have provisionally restored the original status of the claim about the truth value of the sentence 'God exists.' In cases of this kind the second and third steps of the metatheistic enterprise would need to be repeated for the new philosophical account of the relevant crucial concepts that determine the meaning of the sentence that is identified as part of the meaning of the sentence 'God exists.'

It turns out that the metatheist's enterprise is complicated by the fact that the second step of that enterprise must be repeated for each and every identifiable *version* of theism. The second step of the metatheistic enterprise must be repeated for each different version of theism because the second step is relative to and dependent on the *particular* version of theism under consideration. The metatheist's attempt to discover or uncover the assumed meaning of the sentence 'God exists' is relative to and dependent on a *particular* account provided by a *given* theist or group of theists for a *selected* set of properties regarded by *that* theist or group of theists as necessary properties of a divine being.

There are two consequences of the fact that the second step of the metatheist's enterprise is relative and dependent in this way. First, the metatheistic enterprise would never be finished until *all* versions of theism had been analyzed. Second, the third step of the metatheist's enterprise never provides conclusive reasons for making an absolute judgment about theism unless the metatheist can identify a partial meaning for the sentence 'God exists' that is demonstrably necessary for *all* versions of theism. This is true because the metatheist's attempt to establish some ground for making a judgment about the truth value of the sentence 'God exists' is also relative and dependent. The third step of the metatheistic enterprise is relative to and dependent on the second step of discovering or uncovering the assumed meaning of the sentence 'God exists' and the second step is itself relative to and dependent on a *particular* account provided by a *given* theist or group of theists for a *selected* set of properties regarded by *that* theist or group of theists as necessary properties of a divine being. In short, the third step of the metatheistic enterprise is relative to and dependent on the second step and the second step is itself relative to and dependent on the *version* of theism under consideration.

The obvious consequence of these considerations is that the result of applying the metatheistic enterprise is a result that would hold only with respect to a particular version of theism unless that result was entailed by a partial meaning of the sentence 'God exists' that is demonstrably necessary for all versions of theism. For example, assume as a first case that 'a being who created everything from nothing exists' is a partial meaning assigned to the sentence 'God exists' by a group of theists known as Godists. Suppose also that Godists are famous for their unorthodox account of the concept of creation out of nothing and that this unorthodox account is both common and peculiar to Godists. If a metatheist were to demonstrate that the sentence 'God exists' is false because the sentence 'a being who created everything from nothing exists' is itself false by virtue of the concept of creation out of nothing as that concept is explicated by Godists, this result of applying the metatheistic enterprise would hold only with respect to the version of theism known as Godism and to no other version of theism. This metatheistic critique would *not* be a critique of all versions of theism because, as we assumed, the unorthodox meaning assigned to the sentence 'a being who created everything from nothing exists' is peculiar to Godism and not acknowledged by any other version of theism.

Now assume as a second case that 'an omnipotent being exists' is a partial meaning assigned to the sentence 'God exists' and that it is demonstrably necessary that *all* versions of theism acknowledge this partial meaning. Assume also that some critic of theism argues that the paradox of omnipotence falsifies the sentence 'an omnipotent being exists' and, hence, falsifies the sentence 'God exists.' If a metatheist were to demonstrate that the paradox of omnipotence does not in fact falsify the sentence 'an omnipotent being exists' because of what is entailed by the concept of omnipotence, the result of applying the metatheistic enterprise would hold not just with respect to some version of theism or other, but with respect to all versions of theism.[3] This metatheistic defense would be a defense of all versions of theism because, as we assumed, 'an omnipotent being exists' is a partial meaning of the sentence 'God exists' that is demonstrably necessary for *all* versions of theism. So, it should be clear that the result of applying the metatheistic enterprise is a result that holds only with respect to a particular version of theism unless that result is entailed by a partial meaning of the sentence 'God exists' that is demonstrably necessary for *all* versions of theism.

What I have been calling the metatheistic enterprise is reflected in the articles in this volume and is a development of the research and writing which produced those articles. What I have referred to as the doctrine of metatheism is the consequence of the philosophical analysis involved in the actual practice of the metatheistic enterprise. So, there is a temporal order and a procedural order. From a procedural point of view one would practice the metatheistic enterprise as a result of being convinced by the assumptions of the doctrine of metatheism. From a temporal point of view the practice of the metatheistic enterprise and the philosophical analysis it involves came first and suggested the doctrine of metatheism that is the consequence of that enterprise. Had the doctrine and the enterprise been fully worked out in advance of these articles there may well have been a concluding paragraph added to each piece relating the article and its conclusions to both the doctrine of metatheism and the metatheistic enterprise.

For example, "The Hidden Assumption in the Paradox of Omnipotence" and "Descartes on God's Ability to Do the Logically Impossible" are metatheistic defenses of theism. The former is a defense of all versions of theism which hold that 'an omnipotent being exists' is at least part of the meaning of the sentence 'God exists.' The latter is a defense of any version of theism which subscribes to the view that 'a creator of the eternal truths exists' is part of the meaning of the sentence 'God exists.' On the other hand, though I have not demonstrated it, I am convinced that the partial meaning assigned to the sentence 'God exists,' discussed by inference in "Unjustified Evil and God's Choice," is a partial meaning required by all versions of theism. I am convinced of this because I am convinced that 'a being exists who created everything and who had no need to create anything' is a partial meaning for the sentence 'God exists' that is required by all versions of theism. I think that this partial meaning is required by all versions of theism because if it were not then something would exist that is independent of God. Either a being or some higher principal determining God's creative activity would exist independently of God and this would raise serious questions about whether or not God is an adequate object of worship. What is needed is a demonstration that this partial meaning is required by all versions of theism and this would involve an analysis of the concept of being worthy of worship or the concept of an adequate object of worship. Such an analysis is needed but it is also very complicated and must await another time. So, I leave it to the reader to work out how each of the articles in this volume is in fact related to the doctrine of metatheism and the metatheistic enterprise.

NOTES

1. This view is expressed frequently in Augustine's writings, but consult *On True Religion,* chapter 14, 28 and chapter 18, 35 as well as *The Confessions,* Book 13, chapter 4. The account provided by Aquinas can be found in the *Summa Theologia,* I, question 5 and in the *Summa Contra Gentiles,* Book One, chapters 37 and 38 as well as Book Three, chapter 21, paragraph 4.

2. This view was expressed in letters to me from George Mavrodes and Alvin Plantinga. Both of these letters were responses to the argument presented in my article "Unjustified Evil and God's Choice" and Plantinga's letter was an answer to a request authorized by the editor for a response from him to appear in the same issue of the journal as my article.

3. My article "The Hidden Assumption in the Paradox of Omnipotence" (see pp. 93 to 95 of this volume) contains a metatheistic defense of just this kind for all versions of theism which maintain that 'an omnipotent being exists' is a partial meaning of the sentence 'God exists.'

21

The Problem of Evil and Augustine's Account of Human Free Will and Divine Grace

There is an enormous amount of human suffering in the world. Some of it is caused by things or events beyond human control such as viruses, plants, earthquakes, floods, droughts, storms, and the like. This kind of human suffering is usually referred to as *natural evil*. Much human suffering, though, is intentionally caused by the free acts of finite agents such as muggers, murderers, rapists, slave traders, Hitler, and the like. This kind of human suffering is usually referred to as *moral evil*. There is a third kind of evil often discussed by medieval thinkers, but largely neglected in modern discussions. This third kind of evil is the *wickedness* of finite agents who freely *desire* to violate some moral principle, or freely *elect* to bring about some state of affairs that they do not need to bring about and that they know will cause human suffering if they do bring it about. This I shall call *volitional evil*.

Although it is not their exclusive concern, most modern critics of traditional Judaeo-Christian theism commonly cite the existence of moral evil in the world as the fact causing the greatest problem for some of the central doctrines of traditional theism. The problematic doctrines are the doctrine that God is omniscient, the doctrine that God is omnibenevolent, and the doctrine that God is omnipotent. These modern critics of traditional theism think that at least one of these doctrines is falsified by the fact

This paper was written during a sabbatical leave from SUNY College at Buffalo for the academic year 1989–1990.

that much human suffering in the world is intentionally caused by the free acts of finite agents. According to these critics, at least one of these doctrines must be false because if God is omniscient then He knows that there is human suffering in the world, moreover, if God is omnibenevolent and omnipotent then He would want to prevent and could prevent the human suffering in the world. Since there is human suffering in the world that is intentionally caused by the free acts of finite agents and is not prevented by God, either God does not know about it because He is not omniscient, or God does not want to prevent it because He is not omnibenevolent, or God is unable to prevent it because He is not omnipotent. In other words, since there is human suffering in the world intentionally caused by the free acts of finite agents, either it is false that God is omniscient, or it is false that God is omnibenevolent, or it is false that God is omnipotent.

In spite of this problem cited by their critics, many traditional Judaeo-Christian theists think that the problem of evil can be solved by stating the reason God has for not preventing moral evil and showing that that reason does not falsify the claims that God is omniscient, that God is omnibenevolent, or that God is omnipotent. The attempt to state what *reason* God has for not preventing moral evil in the world is usually called a theodicy. Some writers have recently tried to make a distinction between a *theodicy* and what they call a *defense*. According to these writers a defense is the attempt to state what *might possibly be the reason* God has for not preventing moral evil in the world. This alleged distinction, though, is at best nominal. It is nominal because a theodicy is trivially a defense by the principle that whatever is actual is possible. Moreover, a defense is nothing more than a conditional theodicy because it involves the claim that if certain things are true about possible worlds, then God's reason for not preventing moral evil is that He cannot prevent moral evil and His inability to do so is consistent with His omniscience, omnibenevolence, and omnipotence. For the purposes of the present discussion the term 'theodicy' is adequate for talking about the attempt by traditional theists to find a solution to the problem of evil.

One attempt at developing an acceptable theodicy rests on the claim that God is not responsible for the human suffering in question because it is brought about by the *free* acts of finite agents and such a theodicy is called a *free will* theodicy. According to the proponents of a free will theodicy God could have prevented the moral evil of human suffering intentionally brought about by the free acts of finite agents, but only by preventing all free acts intended to cause human suffering. In order to prevent all these free acts, it is held, God would have had to create beings who are *unable* to perform, or *unable* to choose to perform, acts intended to result in human suffering rather than create beings who are *able* to perform and *able* to choose to perform such acts. In other words, God could have prevented moral evil in the world *only* by creating automata instead of creating free finite agents.

At this juncture in their response to the problem of evil the proponents of a free will theodicy (as well as the proponents of a free will "defense") either state or assume what I call the principle of *divine preference*. This principle is that a world of free finite agents who are responsible for their own acts and who intentionally cause human suffering is *better* than a world of automata who never act wrongly because they are unable to choose between acting rightly and acting wrongly or who, in some other way, never act wrongly by some kind of necessity. So, it is argued, since a world of free finite agents responsible for their own acts is *better* than a world of automata who act by some kind of necessity, God created a world of free finite agents *because* it is better than a world of automata and He created this world by virtue of His omniscience, omnibenevolence, and omnipotence.

The conclusion of all this is that it is not God who is responsible, but, rather, the free finite agents themselves who are responsible for the moral evil of human suffering. So, it is claimed, the moral evil of human suffering intentionally caused by the free acts of finite agents does not falsify the claim that God is omniscient, the claim that God is omnibenevolent, or the claim that God is omnipotent. One of the main points of this reasoning is supposed to be that these claims about God's knowledge, goodness, and power are not falsified by the fact of moral evil in the world because God's reason for not preventing the moral evil in question is that He would have had to create a world *inferior* to the one He did create in order to prevent the moral evil. In fact, given this line of reasoning, if God had prevented moral evil by creating a world inferior to the one He did make, that very act of creation would have falsified one of these claims about God's knowledge, goodness, and power. These are the central points of a free will theodicy intended to resolve the problem of evil.

Augustine recognizes a version of the problem of evil and proposes a version of the free will theodicy as a solution to the problem. However, the version of the problem acknowledged by Augustine is not the version of the problem cited by the modern critics of traditional theism. Instead,

Augustine subscribes to a rather grotesque view about evil and human suffering. Augustine does not think, as modern critics of traditional theism do, that human suffering is something that ought to be prevented by an omniscient, omnibenevolent, and omnipotent divine agent. For Augustine, human suffering is not an evil (though he does concede that it seems to be evil to the sufferers) and it is not an evil by virtue of two of the many doctrines to which he subscribes. The first doctrine is that no nature which is less than divine can be hurt unjustly.[1] The second doctrine is that whatever is just cannot be evil.[2] It follows from the first doctrine that human suffering is just. From the second doctrine it follows that human suffering is not evil.

I call his view on the subject of human suffering grotesque because, on his view of divine omnibenevolence, absolutely no example or quantity of human suffering would count as a counterexample to God's goodness and it follows from his view that the heirs of Adam endure no more suffering than what they merit. If the critics of traditional theism were to cite the human suffering of the black victims of the notorious slave traders as cases of human suffering that ought to be prevented by an omniscient, omnibenevolent, and omnipotent being such as God is purported to be, then Augustine would reply that, as with all cases of human suffering, the human suffering endured by the victims of the black slave traders was just and good. It is just and good because no one suffers unjustly and slavery is among the just penalties for sin.[3] For Augustine these victims suffered no more than what they merited and, presumably, so did the victims of the Nazi holocaust. So, for Augustine human suffering is not an evil and, although human suffering is a fact, it is not a fact that requires the traditional Judaeo-Christian theist to forfeit the claim that God is omniscient, omnibenevolent, and omnipotent.

Human suffering, on Augustine's view, is the just penalty for the original sin perpetrated by Adam in the paradise of Eden.[4] For Augustine, evil consists in the original sin of Adam for which we all bear guilt. Since the original sin consisted in forsaking God and falling from His grace instead of remaining in God's grace, evil is the wicked will of Adam to which we are all heirs.[5] On this account of human suffering and evil, the only fact that could be cited as falsifying the theistic claim that God is omniscient, omnibenevolent, and omnipotent is the alleged fact that Adam had the evil desire to forsake God and fall from His grace. Given this particular account of volitional evil the problem of evil for Augustine is the problem of stating what reason an omniscient, omnibenevolent, and omnipotent God had for not preventing Adam from being evil.[6] Instead of addressing the general problem of the moral evil of human suffering as modern theodicists do, Augustine addresses the specific problem of the volitional evil of Adam's original sin which consisted in forsaking God and falling from His grace. Augustine's version of the free will theodicy is his answer to this version of the problem of evil.

As modern theodicists do at this point, Augustine appeals to free will as the basis for formulating the reason God has for not preventing evil in the world. In this case, though, the reason being formulated is the reason God has for not preventing Adam's volitional evil of choosing to forsake God and fall from His grace. Augustine's claim is that even though God created Adam, God is not responsible for the evil in question because of two facts. First, Adam was created perfect by God.[7] Second, the volitional evil of original sin was brought about by a free act of Adam.[8] In short, God is not responsible for the evil in question because the volitional evil of choosing to forsake God and fall from His grace was, according to Augustine, brought about by the free act of a finite agent just as the moral evil of human suffering is, according to modern theodicists, brought about by the free acts of finite agents.

On Augustine's account, God could have indeed prevented the volitional evil of original sin perpetrated by Adam's free choice. In order to prevent Adam's free choice God could have created Adam as a being unable to make the free choice in question rather than create Adam as a being capable of making the crucial free choice. In other words, God could have prevented Adam's volitional evil by creating an automaton instead of creating a free finite agent. Corresponding to the moves of the modern theodicists, Augustine also holds the principle of divine preference.[9] On his view, a world with Adam as a free finite agent responsible for his own choices is *better* than a world with Adam as an automaton unable to make free choices. On the basis of this principle, God created a world with Adam as a responsible and free finite agent *because* it is better than a world with Adam as an automaton. It is concluded from all this that it is not God who is responsible, but, rather, Adam who is responsible for the volitional evil of original sin. So, according to Augustine's line of reasoning, Adam's volitional evil of choosing to forsake God and fall from His grace does not falsify the claim that God is omniscient, the claim that God is omnibenevolent, or the claim that God is omnipotent.

In spite of these similarities between a modern free will theodicy and Augustine's free will theodicy, Augustine's version suffers from two problems not shared by the modern version. The first difficulty with Augustine's version results from the account of human free will that is explicated in his treatise *On Rebuke and Grace*. Among his claims about human free will that occur in this work Augustine has two central principles.[10] His first principle on human free will is that free will is sufficient for evil. Presumably, this is to be understood to mean that doing evil *consists in* freely choosing to do evil whether or not the freely choosing agent actually brings about the evil that was chosen. Augustine's second principle on human free will is that free will is insufficient for good unless it is aided by God. Presumably, this is to be understood to mean that doing good requires *both* that an agent freely choose to bring about a good *and* that the agent receive the aid of God. In his *Retractations* Augustine articulates a third principle on human free will. His third principle on human free will is that the good use of free will is itself numbered among the great goods.[11] Augustine makes it clear in his work on rebuke and grace that remaining in God's grace is the good that Adam should have brought about and that falling from God's grace is the evil that Adam did in fact bring about in original sin. Adam brought about this evil by freely choosing not to remain in God's grace, that is, from Augustine's principle that free will is sufficient for evil it follows that Adam brought about the evil of falling from God's grace by the very act of freely choosing not to remain in God's grace.

So, according to Augustine, remaining in God's grace is a good and Adam should have brought about

(1) The good of remaining in God's grace.

It is at this point that the problem arises for Augustine. In order to bring about (1) Adam had to *choose* to bring about (1). Furthermore, from Augustine's principle that the good use of free will is itself a good it follows that Adam's free *choice* to bring about (1) is itself a good. So, Adam is required to bring about that latter good in order to bring about the good of remaining in God's grace. In other words, in order to bring about (1) it is necessary for Adam to bring about

(2) The good of freely *choosing* to bring about (1).

Now, at this juncture, it might ordinarily be thought that Adam's *act* of freely choosing to remain in God's grace is all that is required for Adam to bring about (2). On Augustine's view of human free will, though, this is not the case. By his second principle on human free will, in order for a finite agent to bring about a good it is required *both* that the finite agent freely will to bring about the good in question and that the finite agent receive the aid of God. So, if (2) is to occur, then it is required *both* that Adam freely *will* to bring about (2) *and* that Adam receive the aid of God.

Again, though, the very act of freely *willing* to bring about (2) is itself a *good* that Adam is required to bring about in order to bring about (2). So, in order to bring about (2) Adam would have been required to bring about

(3) The good of freely *willing* to bring about (2).

Given Augustine's second principle on human free will it is plain that in order to bring about (3) it would be necessary for Adam to freely *resolve* to bring about (3). Moreover, Adam's act of freely *resolving* to bring about (3) is itself a good and Adam is required to bring about that good if he is going to bring about (3). In other words, in order to bring about (3) it would be necessary for Adam to bring about

(4) The good of freely *resolving* to bring about (3).

Again, from Augustine's second principle on human free will it follows that in order to bring about (4) Adam would have been required to freely *elect* to bring about (4). In addition, Adam's act of freely *electing* to bring about (4) is a good. Accordingly, Adam is required to bring about

(5) The good of freely *electing* to bring about (4)

as a necessary condition of his bringing about (4). It follows from all this that in order to bring about (2) Adam would have been required to bring about (3) and in order to bring about (3) Adam would have needed to bring about (4), but in order to bring about (4) it would have been necessary for Adam to bring about (5). Furthermore, this series of good acts of free will that Adam is required to bring about in order to bring about (2) is a series that would continue *ad infinitum*.

The difficulty here is quite plain. In order to bring about (2), the good of freely choosing to remain in God's grace, Adam would have been required to perform an infinite series of acts. Furthermore, if it was necessary for Adam to perform an infinite series of acts in order to bring about this good, then there is no time at which Adam could have brought about this good. In short, there is no time at which Adam could have freely chosen to remain in God's grace. So, Adam fell from God's grace and it was not within his power to do otherwise. According to Augustine's account of the nature of human free will given by God to Adam, Adam fell from grace and *his fall from grace was not the result of an act of his free will.* It follows from this account of human free will that Adam was not responsible for his fall from grace.

On the other hand, in his theodicy Augustine makes two inconsistent claims. The first claim is that human free will was given by God to Adam. The second claim is that by an act of free will Adam chose to forsake God and fell from His grace. The problem is that the first claim entails that Adam's fall from grace is *not,* as we have just seen above, the result of an act of his free will and the second claim entails that Adam's fall from grace *is* the result of an act of his free will. In short, Augustine's version of the free will theodicy entails a contradiction and, so, it does not provide a solution to the problem of evil as Augustine seems to think. Even if Augustine could overcome this problem with his theodicy by providing a different account of the nature of human free will that does not make his theodicy contradictory, there still remains a difficulty.

The second difficulty with Augustine's version of the free will theodicy results from his account of divine grace which is given with his account of human free will in *On Rebuke and Grace.* There Augustine attributes to God two kinds of grace given to man.[12] Both are assumed to be consistent with free will. The first grace is that by which man *would never will* to be evil. The second grace is that by which man *could will never* to be evil. According to Augustine Adam had the second kind of grace but not the first. Given this account of God's grace, God was not limited to the possibilities of creation suggested by Augustine's theodicy. In other words, God was not limited to creating Adam either as an automaton or as a free finite agent who would in fact will to be evil. It follows from Augustine's own account of divine grace that God could have prevented the volitional evil of Adam without sacrificing the good of human free will by creating Adam as a free finite agent who *would never will* to be evil. Moreover, if a world with Adam as a free finite agent who in fact falls from grace is *better* than a world with Adam as an automaton, then surely a world with Adam as a free finite agent who *would never will* to be evil is better still. It seems obvious, then, that God ought to have created the latter world and the fact that He did not falsifies the claim that God is omniscient, omnibenevolent, and omnipotent. In short, Augustine's version of the free will theodicy does not succeed because of his own account of divine grace. Thus, even if Augustine were to modify his account of human free will and thereby eliminate the contradiction in his theodicy, his theodicy would fail.

NOTES

1. Augustine, *The Nature of the Good,* trans. J. H. S. Burleigh, in *Augustine: Earlier Writings,* ed. J. H. S. Burleigh (Philadelphia: The Westminster Press, 1953), p. 329 and p. 336.

2. Augustine, *On Free Will,* trans. J. H. S. Burleigh, in *Augustine: Earlier Writings,* ed. J. H. S. Burleigh (Philadelphia: The Westminster Press, 1953), p. 163.

3. Augustine, *The City of God,* trans. M. Dods, in *Basic Writings of Saint Augustine,* ed. Whitney J. Oates (New York: Random House, 1948), pp. 491–92.

4. Ibid., pp. 584–85.

5. Ibid., pp. 254–55.

6. Augustine, *On Free Will,* p. 185 and p. 213.

7. Ibid., p. 126.

8. Ibid., p. 214.

9. Ibid., p. 180 and p. 191.

10. Augustine, *On Rebuke and Grace,* trans. Robert Ernest Wallis, in *A Select Library of the Nicene and Post-Nicene Fathers of the Christian Church,* vol. 5, ed. Philip Schaff (Grand Rapids: Wm. B. Eerdmans Publishing Company, 1971), p. 484.

11. Augustine, *The Retractations,* trans. Mary Inez Bogan, in *The Fathers of the Church,* vol. 60 (Washington, D.C.: The Catholic University of America Press, 1968), pp. 38–39.

12. Augustine, *On Rebuke and Grace,* pp. 484–85.

Selected Bibliography of Related Material

WORKS BY RICHARD R. LA CROIX

Proslogion II and III: A Third Interpretation of Anselm's Argument. Leiden, The Netherlands: E. J. Brill, 1972.
"Passmore and Cudworth on the Promise-Keeping Act." *Graduate Review of Philosophy* 5, no. 3 (Spring 1963).

Reviews

"An Essay on a New Philosophy of Nature" by Gaston Reno. *Bibliography of Philosophy* 23, no. 2 (1976).
"Religion in a Religious Age" edited by S. D. Goitein. *Bibliography of Philosophy* 23, no. 2 (1976).
"The Significance of Neoplatonism" edited by R. Baine Harris. *Bibliography of Philosophy* 24, no. 2 (1977).
"Forgotten Truth: The Primordial Tradition" by Huston Smith. *Bibliography of Philosophy* 25, no. 1 (1978).

RESPONSES TO WORKS BY RICHARD R. LA CROIX

Responses to Proslogion II and III

Campbell, Richard. *From Belief to Understanding.* Canberra, Australia: The Australian National University, 1976.

Hopkins, Jasper. *Anselm of Canterbury,* Vol. 4. Toronto and New York: The Edwin Mellen Press, 1976.

Schufreider, Gregory. "The Identity of Anselm's Argument." *The Modern Schoolman* 54, no. 4 (May 1977).

————. *An Introduction to Anselm's Argument.* Philadelphia: Temple University Press, 1978.

Yandell, Keith. "Proslogion II and III: A Third Interpretation of Anselm's Argument by Richard R. La Croix," *The Journal of Value Inquiry* 8, no. 2 (Summer 1974).

Responses to Specific Articles

Colwell, Gary. "Omnipotence and Omniscience." *Sophia* (Australia) 14, no. 2 (July 1975).

Godbey, Jr., John W. "The Incompatibility of Omnipotence and Omniscience." *Analysis* 34, no. 2 (December 1973).

Gregory, Donald R. "Divine Omniprescience and Literary Creativity: Has La Croix Shown Their Incompatibility?" *Religious Studies* 18, no. 1 (March 1982).

Kapitan, Tomis. "Can God Make Up His Mind?" *International Journal for Philosophy of Religion* 43, no. 3 (March 1983).

Mavrodes, George I. "Defining Omnipotence." *Philosophical Studies* (U.S.) 32, no. 2 (August 1977).

Meierding, Loren. "The Impossibility of Necessary Omnitemporal Omnipotence." *International Journal for Philosophy of Religion* 11, no. 1 (Spring 1980).

Peterson, Michael L. "Evil and Inconsistency." *Sophia* (Australia) 18, no. 2 (July 1979).

Podet, Allen Howard. "La Croix's Paradox: An Analysis." *International Journal for Philosophy of Religion* 18, nos. 1–2 (1985).

Quinn, Philip L. "Divine Foreknowledge and Divine Freedom." *International Journal for Philosophy of Religion* 9, no. 4 (1978).

Taliaferro, Charles. "The Magnitude of Omnipotence." *International Journal for Philosophy of Religion* 14, no. 2 (1983).

Teske, Roland J. "Properties of God and the Predicaments in *De Trinitate V.*" *The Modern Schoolman* 59, no. 11 (November 1981).

Wainwright, William J. "Augustine on God's Simplicity: A Reply to Richard La Croix." *The New Scholasticism* 53, no. 1 (Winter 1979).

Wierenga, Edward. "Omnipotence Defined." *Philosophy and Phenomenological Research* 43, no. 3 (March 1983).